Lieutenant Calley
His Own Story

Also by John Sack

The Butcher

From Here to Shimbashi

Report from Practically Nowhere

M

Lieutenant Calley / His Own Story

John Sack

THE VIKING PRESS · NEW YORK

85 B7187

First published in 1971 by The Viking Press, Inc.

625 Madison Avenue, New York, N.Y. 10022

Published simultaneously in Canada by

The Macmillan Company of Canada Limited.

SBN 670-42821-3

Library of Congress catalog card number: 73-153127

Printed in U.S.A.

About half of this book appeared first in *Esquire* in different form. The author is very grateful to Harold Hayes and Don Erickson of *Esquire* for their editorial help.

People will ask me, "Are these words yours or Lieutenant Calley's?" They are Lieutenant Calley's. To try to invent sentences for Calley to acquiescently initial—to try to suborn his perjury would be a rather degenerate enterprise for a reporter, and I wouldn't undertake it. Neither would he.

Instead, I talked to Calley a hundred days. Without exaggeration, I asked him somewhere near ten thousand questions, or one question for each three-fourths of a sentence here. I sought to elicit his past thoughts rather than to inspire newer ones or insinuate mine. His answers on five hundred thousand inches of magnetic tapes and a fiftieth ton of transcripts spared me the only humdrum part of a writer's work: the putting the actual words in. Calley's words, Calley's sentiments, I took apart and I put together as a continuous story. The bubbles of air within it I cut without qualms, and I added facts from the reference shelf if Calley wanted me to. From trial transcripts, I added the

Q-and-A of the four prosecution witnesses who were bodily at the scene with him, or testified so. Aside from them, Calley has little quarrel with the prosecution case. It was mostly prelude—the same language, the same story, a blanket of boredom, to use some phrases by Richard Hammer in *The Court-Martial of Lt. Calley*. The defense case is this whole book.

I liked being with Lieutenant Calley. To me he seemed sensible, intelligent if intelligence lies in the life examined, sensitive, sincere— But enough. His sincerity is crystal clear to anyone who is talking with him. I appeal to the reader not to lose sight of it.　　　　　　—JOHN SACK

Lieutenant Calley
His Own Story

I liked it in South Vietnam. I knew, *I can be killed here,* but I could also be more alive than in America. In Vietnam, I had to live every moment. Say if I had a C-ration can to make dinner out of: I could just sit and say, *God, is this bad,* or I could pull up some onions or some chili peppers and I could make a gourmet meal. It was slower, sure: but I was more excited than if I was spoon-fed in Atlanta. Or say if I was invited out to a Vietnamese home. The food I wouldn't like (I hardly could eat it): still it would be an experience. Which a cocktail party in Georgia isn't.

I really felt, *I belong here.* It may seem ridiculous saying this. Why in the world would a guy just commit himself to South Vietnam? Well, why would a guy commit himself to South Dakota? Why would a guy become a plumber? Or a Professor Einstein? I just knew, *It isn't working here. I'm an American officer and I belong in South Vietnam.* For an Army man, a tour in Vietnam is just twelve months, but I had extended in November, 1968, and I was still there in May, 1969. And then the division called, and I heard that a reassignment from the Department of Army was in. It said,

> CALLEY, WILLIAM L JR 05347602. DEROS Vietnam 30 May 1969. Reassigned to CBR Warfare School, Fort McClellan, Alabama. TDY three days, Office of the Inspector General, Washington, D.C. See special instructions below.

And these said,

> On arrival in CONUS contact Office of the Inspector General, Washington, D.C.

It ran through me, I was going home to a gas school—a chemical, biological, and radiological warfare school at Fort McClellan, Alabama, for some reassignment with the Inspector General's Corps (I had been an insurance investigator once). I figured, I had three days in Washington so I could be briefed about it.

The clerk said, "Or do you want to extend here?"

"I don't know. I'll think about it."

"Okay. And there's a mistake on the orders, apparently. It says you're to leave on 30 May—" Right then was 30 May. "It must be 30 June."

"No hurry." I even kidded the Colonel about it, "I'm on my way today, sir. I better pack up."

"You'll eat whale shit! You ain't going nowhere!"

And seven days after that, I walked into the orderly room. And the first sergeant asked me, "What did you do, Lieutenant? Tear up the officers club?"

"What did I do this time?"

"I don't know, but Division's hot! Who did you piss on, Lieutenant?"

"I don't really know." I borrowed the first sergeant's jeep, and I asked at Division, "What's going on?"

"I don't know, but the Pentagon told us these orders are right." And they gave me my orders, my personnel records, my airplane ticket to Washington, D.C. On a plane in just sixty minutes!

I packed a bag hurriedly, I kissed my cleaning girl's forehead, and I said, "I come right back."

She said, "No no. You will no come back."

I said, "I come right back," and I jumped on a plane to Camranh bay. I checked in, I said, "A bourbon, please," at the officers club, and suddenly there were the MPs shouting, "Lieutenant Calley! Lieutenant Calley!" I got on another plane (I guess I had bumped some GI who really wanted to go) and I was in Washington the next day. I thought, *I'm getting a medal, perhaps.* Or something: it was intriguing, right?

Now, near the Capitol's the Inspector General's Office, and I reported in. And that's when I knew, *Something's wrong.* No one said anything but "Sit down here," and "Sit down here," and "I'll be right with you, Lieutenant Calley." At last a full colonel, I'd say about six foot four (I'm five four and I'm not good at estimating height)—a colonel met me. I didn't like the colonel's bearing much. He wasn't forceful.

He seemed uncomfortable with me. "Lieutenant? This is a Mr. Such-and-Such. A court reporter, and he is taking everything down."

"Well, that's nice. What's going on?"

"Sit down, Lieutenant. This is a formal investigation for the personal use of the Chief of Staff. Do you want an attorney?"

"Do you mind telling me, Colonel: what's going on? I mean do I need an attorney?"

"Do you *think* you need an attorney?"

I think that I slapped the colonel's table. "Well, listen! I'm tired, sir! I've just flown in! *What in the hell's going on?*"

"Sit down, Lieutenant. This is about an operation on 16 March 1968 in or about the village of Mylai Four. At the conclusion of this investigation, you will probably—" No, the colonel said, "You will possibly be charged with murder."

"Do you mean you pulled me out of Vietnam just to tell me—" It seemed like the silliest thing I had heard of. Murder.

"Well, do you want an attorney?"

"Do you think I should have an attorney?"

"Yes, I would have an attorney."

"I'll have an attorney." In a minute they had an attorney for me: a captain.

The colonel said, "I have a few questions for you."

"Well, shoot."

The attorney said, "You shouldn't answer them, I don't think."

"I'll answer anything!"

The attorney said, "Be careful. You can be charged with murder."

"Is that serious?"

The attorney sort of just looked at me. "You can get death for murder."

"Oh, it is serious then." It hadn't filtered in on me, the seriousness of it. Murder: what a preposterous idea. I thought if I wanted to, I could go back to South Vietnam. Tomorrow! Me being dumb, I'd almost told the colonel everything. To include what I thought of the colonel! That he was a prime example why the Army is screwed up, sometimes. And why the Army sometimes can't get a goddamn decent thing done. He couldn't talk to me, that colonel. He stuttered: he had a format and he wouldn't budge from it. As in Vietnam: a GI can't say, "Sit down with me, Mama-san. I'll explain this," a GI just can't communicate with her. Or do anything else but to find, to close with, and to destroy or capture enemy: the infantry's mission. Tell him to pacify them, and he can't understand you. He is awkward. Like the colonel there.

I said, "The way this lawyer is telling it, Colonel, you're out to hang someone, aren't you?"

"No no! I'm not! I'm not! It isn't for me! It's all for the Chief of Staff!"

"You tell the Chief of Staff: if I can help, I'll be glad to. But if you're out to *hang* anyone—stick the investigation sideways between your jaws."

I was upset! I got to my hotel that day (I was at Hospitality House, the Army was paying) and I was—well, extremely hurt. I couldn't understand it. I kept thinking, though. I thought, *Could it be I did something wrong?* I knew that war's wrong. Killing's wrong: I realized that. I had gone to a war, though. I had killed, but I knew, *So did a million others.* I sat there, and I couldn't find the key. I pictured the people of Mylai: the bodies, and they didn't bother me. I had found, I had closed with, I had destroyed the VC: the mission that day. I thought, *It couldn't be wrong or I'd have remorse about it.*

And then, I guess I became afraid. *What if they're right? What if I am a murderer, somehow? What if I am found guilty? What if—* I was afraid to think about it. I stayed afraid till I got here to Fort Benning, Georgia.

Not to Fort McClellan, Alabama. The reason was, I was assigned here by a colonel with the Inspector General's Office. "You'll have a better chance there," the colonel told me. Here everything is infantry, and I would have an infantry jury: a combat-officer jury, and either you've been in Vietnam in combat, or you'll never understand it. You'll say a VC is a Vietnamese man with weapons and a civilian— "He has a house. He works every day. He comes home for dinner. He thinks—ah, good thoughts. A civilian." But if you're ever in combat—well, a combat officer knows that he just can't say, "Who is VC around here?" His enemies, in America are often called civilians. And at Benning the chance that an officer on a court-martial jury did the same thing that I did is damn better than at Fort McClellan or, say, at Fort Houston, Texas. Where all you've got is Wacs and doctors.

In fact, I worked at Benning eighteen months, and I never had an officer down on me. When officers saw the CALLEY over my shirt pocket, they told me, "Saw you on TV the other day! You're looking good," or "I'm behind you all the way," or "I'm with you." It happened each day at the officers club and the deputy commander's office and the PX—

"I'm behind you."

"Thank you."

"How can I help you?"

"Thank you. But you help me just being behind me."

I worked with the deputy commander here. He didn't have a job, really, and I'm not a golfer (and I wouldn't caddy for him) so I hadn't much to do. Every day, I got to his office at eight o'clock with a "Good morning, Mrs. Peterson!" The deputy commander's secretary: and we had coffee together saying, "How are your children?" "How is your girl friend?" "How is—" etcetera, until we both started on *The Columbus Enquirer* and *The Atlanta Journal*. I'm sick of front pages now, and I turned to *B.C.*, *Peanuts*, and *Snuffy Smith*. And to Ann Landers: if I was ambitious, we answered my letters, though. I had 5000 then, about ten of them derogatory to me: "You sonofabitch!" "Our brothers and sisters died in Mylai!" "I hope you're damned!" The others—well, I had letters and letters asking me, "Why are they picking on you? I was in Vietnam also, and one day—" I won't repeat it, though, the Army's in trouble enough as it is. I had letters and letters like,

I served in Korea from June 1953 to August 1954. I heard of many similar incidents.

I'm a retired marine. I spent twenty years in the service of God and Country. I was in two operations in Korea where women and children were killed.

In 1943, 1944, 1945, and 1946 I was a first lieutenant with the 45th Infantry Division. I was witness to many incidents similar to the one you're being held for.

I served in combat in the German war. My fellow soldiers and I did on occasion kill enemy soldiers, civilians, and children. Marquess of Queensberry rules do not prevail in war.

During my duty in Africa we were under orders to shoot the Arabs to keep them from taking our clothes.

I was given the order to seal a cave where a mother and her eleven or twelve children were holed up. This took place in 1944 on the island of Ie Shima.

On Okinawa, I saw men throw grenades on old men and women, figuring what the hell—they're the enemy.

What the hell. I'm positive there were a countless number of people, anywhere you could care to mention, who, in our efforts to liberate a given locale, died. It is inevitable.

Many years ago I had a platoon, and we went through the villages as you and your people had to.

In fact, I had a letter from—God knows who, a colonel from the Spanish-American War. A well-written, a well-spelled, a letter-perfect letter. The colonel said, the Spanish had put the people in concentration camps till the great white father in Washington said, "We'll save you!" And went there, and pounced around, and created havoc, and beat the living hell out of Spain—and put the people in concentration camps. In which the colonel told me: thousands died.

I had letters and letters telling me, "Please visit us," or "Please come for Christmas dinner," to Georgia, Louisiana, Texas, to New York, Nebraska, Oregon. It was flattering: I had letters from the John Birchers and the American Legion *and* the NAACP and the Civil Liberties Union. All of them asking, "How can I help?" And telephone calls from London, England. Once, I had been afraid that if I went shopping in Georgia someone might ask me, "Are you Lieutenant Calley? *Pow*," and take a punch at me. But instead— well, the first time it happened was at Miller's discount store in Columbus. I was there with my girl friend for a can of red paint for my motorboat when a gentleman said, "Are you Lieutenant Calley?" Anne did a 360 circle and practically said, "I'm not with him." But me, I figured, *I'll face it.*

"Yes, I'm Lieutenant Calley."

"I agree with you, Lieutenant. I am behind you all the way. It's a terrible thing when the Army calls it a war crime when it just happens every day. I know what war is! I was in World War II and Korea, and I'm lucky we weren't tried in Korea—"

"Thank you. Thank you. Thank you," I told him. "I have to go." Because what the letters, the telephone calls, the people just did to me was embarrass me. So *what* if a gentleman tells me, "I know you're right," if I am Lieutenant Calley and *I* don't know if I'm right? Often, I thought, *The whole damn war in Vietnam isn't right*. I didn't know if I was someone for Anne to associate with. A hundred murders: if I was found guilty, it would be open season against me. She might be persecuted too: I didn't know, but I didn't impose on Anne if she didn't want me to. Once when her father came, I said, "Hi. I am Rusty Calley." It just didn't register: it never did if I didn't say, "I am First Lieutenant William L. Calley Jr. of Mylai Massacre." That's what the world knew me as. My last name was Massacre: but I said, "Hi. I am Rusty Calley. I've heard so much about you. I'm very glad to meet you."

Her father said, "Hi, Rusty. You've got a lot of big things in Columbus. Now that Lieutenant Calley—!"

Anne said, "Yes."

"You're far enough from him, aren't you, Anne? You're safe?"

"He lives out at Fort Benning."

Myself, I went for a new round of scotches. I didn't know if Anne had acted right. I thought, *What if her father finds out? It will mortify him.*

My own father was so behind me, I got uncomfortable about it. He thought that I was Joe Good Guy and I was completely right and if anyone was derogatory about me, people should jail him. "I listened to So-and-So on the television, and they should jail him!" He didn't *really* listen to So-and-So, or to me either: but he had been having a horrifying time of it. Night and day: newspaper, radio, and TV men outside of his little trailer in Miami. My mother isn't alive, but the TV once got my younger sister at Hialeah high school. "Dawn? Now, what do you think of your brother murdering all of those people over in South Vietnam?" What a hell of a question for a fourteen-year-old. My sister was crying then, "I don't think he would do it—" Jesus, I felt ashamed. I felt, *I'm a lousy bastard, I'm hurting my little sister.* I'd like to have taken her hand and told her, "Let's leave here." She and my father went up to Gainesville, finally. To another school.

It must be a trauma for her. I know: I get self-conscious if TV cameras are on me. I think, *I've a button open, I've a big piece of spinach between my teeth—* My worst time was at the Pentagon with the Peers committee. ABC and NBC and CBS were there, and a hundred newspapermen with Kodaks or whatever they use. All shoving and screaming at me, "Walk slower! Walk slower!" Well, I had many letters telling me, "Keep smiling." My attorney told me, "But don't be cheerful: don't be like you've won a prize," and my Army attorney told me, "Be sad. Be like they're torturing you." In fact, I was cheerful that day. A girl from my high school homeroom had written me, "Any time you're in Washington come by," and I had hoped to have dinner with her, her husband, and her three children. She wouldn't ask, "What happened in Mylai, Lieutenant," and I wouldn't have to embarrass her, "I can't talk about it." I'd had to refuse almost all of the invitations to Georgia, Louisiana, Texas, and elsewhere in America.

Anyhow, I was in Washington, and I could see all the TV and newspapermen on the Pentagon steps. I joked in the limousine about it, "I guess there will be a parade here." I jumped out, I started up through the microphones, and I think that a TV correspondent started it.

"Lieutenant Calley! Did you really kill all those women and children?"

"Lieutenant Calley! How does it feel to kill women and children?"

"Lieutenant Calley! Are you sorry you couldn't have killed more women and children?"

"Lieutenant Calley! If you could go back to kill more women and children—"

I busted into the Pentagon. I took the fifth amendment with the Peers committee, and I told a colonel there, "I don't care for that crowd again." We left by a janitor's room, a war room, an iron stairway, and another door.

My trial was set for November, 1970, and I got jumpy as November got closer. I went out to restaurants, and I heard people say, "It's Lieutenant Calley!" "Where?" "There!" I was afraid that I'd step on Anne's foot, and Anne would scream and I'd jump and Anne would hit a waiter and I'd have a bowl of tomato soup on me: I exaggerate, but I couldn't sleep much. I'd lie awake listening, and pop! A natural sound, but I would jump up and turn a light on. And think, *An assassin,* I didn't know who. A man trying to get in the newspapers, maybe. I heard sort of a batting once: of someone trying to get in the front screen door. I opened the door: nothing. I closed it, I had a cigarette and it started again, a batting sound. I went outside and I saw it: a moth, it was caught inside of the front screen door.

I had paranoid fears. I went to the bathroom once and I thought, *Someone's here,* I looked back of the shower curtain, even. I thought, *It won't surprise me if I wake up one morning and I am a babbling idiot. It won't surprise me.* I felt I was in a carnival there, a man everyone was throwing pies at. I had a telephone answering service and a secretary now, and I asked myself, *Is this really me?* I had four marriage proposals, I had some locks of little girls' hair, and I had letters like "Do you like to dance?" "To kiss?" "To park?" One day, I was in the deputy commander's office and a captain said, "Gee. What is it you're doing?" God, what *is* it I'm doing? I was signing autographs. Two hundred people wrote me, "I enclose a self-addressed envelope and a cover of *Time*. Please autograph it." I didn't have the vaguest idea why someone wanted this. To hang next to Hitler? Or hang next to Santa Claus? I read the Calley stories and I said, *Gee, I should go to the school yard, and I should beat up the little kids*. I was in a windstorm, and a thousand pieces of paper swirled around me.

A psychiatrist called: an Army psychiatrist. To ask if I wanted a psychiatric evaluation.

"I think I'm balanced enough," I said.

"I think you're balanced too."

"I'm balanced right now," I continued. "But when it's November—"

Believe me, I *would* be bananas then if I didn't cease to be "Calley" those days. I lived in a cage, and if I felt, *I'm running around it, I'm batting my brains out, I can't escape it*, I did escape by getting away to Atlanta or New York City. I wasn't recognized if I didn't wear a uniform with a CALLEY tag or a T-shirt with a picture of Mylai on it. On Earth Day, I walked twenty blocks on Fifth avenue, and I didn't hear one "It's Lieutenant Calley!" I ate in New York City at Sardi's, the Russian Tea Room, the Right Bank, the Brasserie, the Plaza, the Algonquin, and the Fountain Café in Central Park, and I wasn't stared at except at Bradley's, in Greenwich Village. By a girl sitting sort of catty-corner from me. I thought, *Oh gosh, she recognizes me,* except it was simply a hooker out to solicit me. People think if I'm not a big hairy monster with an M-16 slung over me, I can't be Lieutenant Calley. Not if I haven't a big stick to beat pregnant women with.

So—I would go to Atlanta wearing a three-piece suit. I took in as much as I could of the theater, like *Hello Dolly*. I went to art galleries saying, "That's nice," or "That's crap, and I don't care if they call it *Mona Lisa*," I am that type of person. In April, I went to New York City, and I saw *Hair* and *Oh! Calcutta!* The music I loved. The nudity didn't shock me: Jesus, was it supposed to? Except that in *Hair* they had a shocking scene, and I was extremely offended by it. An actor in *Hair*, he wrapped himself with an American flag as though it was nothing but a rag to clothe himself with. He made a mockery out of it. He sang something such as "Screw the American flag," and he walked on it, stomped on it, dragged it, etcetera, and I just gritted my teeth. I have pride in America, and I hate someone making a slant against it. Sure, it has many flaws. It has made booboos, if you would call them that: I prefer not to. Mistakes. There is too much poverty here. We have to have integration. This war in Vietnam is ridiculous: but I'm an American, and I won't curse it. I won't just say, "It's horrible." What we have in America with its horrors still is the best there is. For what would we have without it? Chaos.

Maybe if I were President, I could change things. Till then, I'm like anyone else: I'll carry America's orders out. For that's what the Army is: a chisel, it has to keep sharp and let the American people use it. If the people say, "Go wipe out South America," the Army will do it. Majority rules, and if a majority tells me, "Go to South Vietnam," I will go. If it tells me, "Lieutenant Calley," or "Rusty Calley," or "Whatever, go massacre one thousand communists," I will massacre one thousand communists. But—I won't advocate it. I'm against massacre, and I won't preach it: I won't be a hypocrite for it. Or maybe *that* is a hypocrite, but I'll do as I'm told to. I won't revolt. I'll put the American people above my own conscience, always. I'm an American citizen.

It's odd about war crimes. We seem to have tried people only if they've lost the war. Vietnam: it may be a sign we've lost it, I wouldn't know. After eighteen months, I went on trial in November in "Calley hall," a courthouse at Fort Benning, Georgia. Up front there would be an Army judge. The jury of Army officers would be on the left-hand side. In back would be thirty seats for TV and newspapermen, twenty for spectators, five for me. I had promised some to my attorney's wife, my Army attorney's wife, and the prosecutor's wife.

The trial: we didn't think in November that it would be four months long. The jury itself took us three days, though. We went through twenty-five officers, most of them prejudiced for me: not personally, but against the Army for trying me. A captain, "It seemed to me, *Somebody was out to railroad somebody.*" A major, "I personally, I didn't think it was right." A lieutenant colonel was most outspoken. His face was hard, tired, weary, worn: I thought of Johnny Cash. And disgusted, as though he had thought, *We're spending thousands of dollars beating the young lieutenant over the goddamn head. The same as we're doing in Vietnam right now.* He came on very decisive.

"Colonel, is your belief prejudicial to the defendant?"

"No."

"Let's put it the other way. Is it prejudicial to the government?"

"Yes."

A full colonel said, "Over there, we never knew who was the enemy, really. A little old twelve-year-old would come up, take your chewing gum, and the next minute drop a grenade." He was to be the jury's president, that man. But the prosecutor had a peremptory challenge. And challenged him.

One of those twenty-five officers said he knew other purported massacres. "Of a similar nature?"

"Of a similar nature."

"Did you ever discuss it with fellow officers?"

"Yes sir. Not only the Mylai incident but similar incidents."

"You were in sympathy with Lieutenant Calley?"

"Yes sir."

"Are you in sympathy with him now?"

"Yes sir."

"You are not in sympathy with the government?"

"No sir."

"I direct your attention to 25 September 1970. Do you recall the order appointing you?" As a possible juror.

"Yes sir."

"Do you recall that you and a lieutenant colonel broke into laughter? And there was some mention that Calley should be promoted?"

"He had enough time—"

He went too far, I believe. It didn't surprise me, though, so many officers being for me. They're veterans, and I think they saw in me, themselves. I once saw an open letter to President Nixon,

Mr. President:

I protest the court-martial of Lt. William L. Calley, Infantry. You, Sir, I and our nation must share the guilt of Vietnam. Calley is being tried by all conscience-stricken citizens, who see him as a reflection of themselves.

I read that, and it just turned a key inside me. If it's true, I had an obligation to everyone in America: *I must be a reflection they'll want to look at.* The guilt itself: I could do nothing about it, Mylai had happened and it would have to stand pat. But there's more to America than war, I knew, and I should try to reflect that too. I should reflect this so Americans could say, "We are good people, too. We aren't tyrants: we try, we make errors, we do things wrong, but we will change and go on." The guilt would hurt, but I should reflect every part of America's people. Because they're a good and a great and a wonderful people.

I had a tremendous responsibility. If that letter's true, if I was a mirror, really, for America, I had to be very honest now, to tell everything there was of Mylai, to give everyone straight turkey with no Christmas dressing with it. I had a greater responsibility than the prosecutor did. I couldn't say, "I didn't do it." I couldn't bring in a GI, give him a decent dinner, give him a witness fee to testify coming and going for me. "Calley's the greatest thing there was. He was Christ walking over the rice paddies—" No, that isn't honest, it isn't what a court in America should be. I was like someone high on a cliff in Acapulco. I could back out ("No, I didn't do it!"). Or could be brave and say, *I'll give her a jump today*. And if I missed the Pacific when the wave's coming in, I'd die and I'd have people say of me, "He was a good ole boy." Or else, "He was an ass: except he had fortitude, and he would do anything once."

It sounded exciting: but I had some secret moments, *I'm not strong enough, I'm not brave enough, I don't really want to go through with it. I can't reflect continuously.* I thought I might cry if the prosecutor said, "He killed a hundred people there." On the trial day, I hadn't slept. I got dressed, I drove to "Calley hall," and I sat down there: I was uptight. I didn't know if a gavel would hit me or— I didn't want to get emotional, though. I knew if I was just dignified, it was better than if I became a babbling idiot like in Chicago: the Chicago Seven. And everyone said, "If that's how we are, to hell with us."

I knew, *I'll destroy my dignity if I'm indignant today*, and I kept composure this way: I wrote. I wrote on a white lined pad,

> My largest fear now is if I'll be able to keep control. There is a tremous [I meant tremendous] amount of fear going through me. I'm starting to shake. I'm trying to reconcile myself that I'm not the first to be going through this. But it doesn't help.

I wrote about the jury beneath it.

> Colonel Ford. A slightly overweight staff officer who hasn't had combat duty [for twenty-five years] and has never been to Vietnam.

> Major McIntosh—

And that's when the prosecutor began. A captain.

"Gentlemen, I'd like to tell you a little bit about Mylai Four. We want you to *be* there, and we will try to put you there on 16 March 1968. The village of Mylai Four is located in Quangngai province—"

I listened and I became relaxed now. I knew, *He can't hurt me*, the captain could have no idea of Mylai or of what happened there. He had never been to Vietnam: to war anywhere, and he was so dissociated from it. He said I had done premeditated murder there. It's true: I sat up with sergeants in the wee hours of March 16, 1968, and I plotted to kill those people in Mylai Four. I filled up the cartridge clips, and god! How premeditated can you get? Of course, in Vietnam we called it a combat assault.

"At seven-thirty," the captain went on, "the helicopters set on the western side of Mylai the accused and the first platoon. They disembarked, but they didn't receive any fire. They found the village undefended. They found women, found children, found old men: none of them armed. Some of them still eating breakfast. So the accused's platoon began to gather these up. These unarmed men, women, children, *babies*, were taken to the southern side of the village by PFC Paul B. Meadlo, Spec Four Dennis I. Conti. The accused directed, 'Take care of these people.' The accused left. Meadlo and Conti guarded the men, the women, the children, the babies. Calley returned. 'Why haven't you taken care of these people?' 'We *have* taken care of them. Guarded them.' 'I mean kill them. Waste them.' And with full bursts of automatic fire, Meadlo and Calley shot those people, those unarmed unresisting—"

He just didn't understand it, the captain. Killing people in war's something new? Now what in the hell *else* is war than killing people? And destroying their homes and their farms and their way of life: that's war! And who in the hell is hurt besides civilians? I sat and I heard the captain talk and I could almost cry: I thought of the thousands of men, thousands of women, thousands of children, thousands of babies slaughtered in Vietnam, the bodies rotting away. The captain didn't seem to know about them. I did: I had been to Vietnam.

I had joined the Army in July, 1966. I had been in insurance then: I'd investigate if a $100,000 home was a $100,000 home or a $100 shanty. At times, I'd find if I got past the CONDEMNED signs that the $100,000 home was in six feet of water, and I'd take a picture and say, "House submerged." I had been doing this in New Orleans, Houston, and San Francisco (I lived uphill from the hippies there) and I suddenly heard from my draft board in Miami. It wrote me: I wasn't there and I had to go to Miami to answer why. All right, I was tired of California anyhow. I was lonely, and I tooled across the country till in Albuquerque the water pump for my Buick busted. It meant that I was broke too. I couldn't make Miami now: I had $4.80 left.

I went to an Army recruiter there. "My damn draft board wants me. How about wiring them, I need money?"

"The draft boards don't work that way."

"Well, what am I going to do?"

"Well—"

I guess he was low on his monthly quota. A recruiter's a salesman, really: he hasn't the most desirable product but he is trying like hell. The recruiter in Albuquerque was—oh, about six foot two, an American high school hero. He had those cardboards behind him, a Wac and an Army nurse. He told me I should enlist.

"What can I do in the Army three years?"

"Oh, we'll find a place for you! Is there something you'll like?"

"Yeah, to get to Miami to talk to my draft board."

"But what about airborne ranger?"

"What's that?"

"That's someone jumps out of airplanes and—"

"No man! I'd rather sit in an air-conditioned office. The guy over there: what is he?"

"A clerk."

"Okay, I'll be a clerk."

"Okay." And ten minutes later, I was a clerk trainee, and I was told I was very proud to be in the US Army.

Well, I was destitute, remember. I had no qualms about the Army, I grew up with people telling me, *It's something you do. You serve* (and I think if you join the Army to question it, you're wrong). I took basic training at Fort Bliss, Texas, and I went to clerical school at Fort Lewis, Washington. And in March, 1967, I went to Fort Benning, Georgia, to Fort Benning School for Boys. That's what we called the officer candidate school here, and we had to learn the "alma mater" the first day in.

> From the banks of Chattahoochie
> To the shores of—trala troys

I forget it,

> Stands our stately alma mater,
> Benning School for Boys.
> Ever forward, never backward,
> To the port of embarkation—

I can't remember it. Call it harassment, but I learned at OCS if I try I can do almost anything. OCS taught that to me. I did an obstacle course once: I was a POW, supposedly, and if I didn't escape over the electrified water and a wall twelve feet high, I would die. Solution: I was thrown over! Four other officer candidates threw me. And shouted to me, "You sonofabitch, make it," I grabbed the twelve foot wall and I made it. Even the pogie bait parties at OCS gave me more confidence. Now, pogie bait is just anything that is not prepared by the government in a government messhall by government-employed personnel: that is not served on a steel tray. Coke, candy, pizza, anything sweet, or anything else: at OCS it was pogie bait, and it was strictly taboo. It was daring to have ourselves a pogie bait party: it was dangerous, but if you're ever at OCS you *try*. It meant sneaking two hundred pizzas in without getting caught.

How? Well, right before taps we took garbage out. And when the trash, wastepaper, dirt, etcetera, had been dumped out, we had twelve empty cans to carry the pizzas back to the barracks in. What's ridiculous was, we devoured them in seconds flat (the record: an eighth of a second) and we just couldn't enjoy it. *Slurp*, and we would be spraying the barracks with Right Guard. But a few hundred pizzas in a room smelling of Johnson's paste wax—a deodorant wouldn't do. A tac officer could be miles away, and he would know it, *Pizza! I have to take immediate action.* If we were lucky: if we had a big inspection due, he sent us into the shower rooms. Has anyone taken a shower eating a pizza pie? It is so—*blah,* we just gagged: when we were lucky, remember. If not, "Gee, you love pizza, don't you, Candidate Calley. Why not just rub it all on your bed-sheets?" And that's what I'd do: rub pizza on all of my bed-sheets and pillowcases so I could wallow in it. And then, "Gee, Candidate Calley. That guy: he seems to love pizza too. Why not throw him a pizza?" Meaning right in his face. Oh, they would let us—*make* us, have pizza fights till we reeked of it, the walls, the floors, the ceilings would just be annihilated: ruined. Till at three in the morning, "All right. The pogie bait party's over. Lights out." So that's when the real confidence course would be: with three hours to rev-eille. We had to clean the sheets, clean the walls, clean the floors (and I mean spit-shined clean) and clean ourselves. In the dark!

One thing we were taught at OCS for twenty years we had thought was bad. To kill, and a sergeant in gym shorts and a T-shirt taught it. We sat around, and he kicked an-other man in the kidney: a few inches lower, really, or this could be a lethal kick. It was just gruesome: a *POP,* and I thought, *Oh god. No one can live through that.* He really kicked, or he flipped a man with karate and *WHAM*: he would show us the follow-up. And stomp on him right be-tween the eyes: pretend to, and push his nose right into his brain. Or stomp on his solar plexus: his ribcage, to push splinters into his lungs. And then stomp on his heart to smash it. The sergeant taught how to use those—what is it? A garotte? Like a jungle vine: to get it around a man's neck immediately. He said don't slit a man's throat if you don't want a sound: an *ughughugh* sucking sound, and don't stab a man in the back anytime. A back has so many muscles, you'll never get a bayonet back out. A good place to stab a man from behind is down through the shoulder, the sergeant said: the left shoulder, preferably, where the heart is, that's how to kill someone best. We never became proficient, though. We did better at cleaning rifles: an M-16 is less gruesome to kill someone with. We thought, *We will go to Vietnam and be Audie Murphys. Kick in the door, run in the hooch, give it a good burst*—kill. And get a big kill ratio in Vietnam. Get a big kill count.

One thing at OCS was nobody said, "Now, there will be innocent civilians there." Oh sure, there will in Saigon. In the secure areas, the Vietnamese may be clapping the way the French in the '44 newsreels do, "Yay for America!" But we would be somewhere else: be in VC country. It was drummed into us, "Be sharp! On guard! As soon as you think these people won't kill you, ZAP! In combat you haven't friends! You have enemies!" Over and over at OCS we heard this, and I told myself, *I'll act as if I'm never secure. As if everyone in Vietnam would do me in. As if everyone's bad.* I went from OCS to Hawaii: to Charlie company, First battalion, Twentieth infantry, and I still didn't hear of innocent civilians. All autumn we landed on beaches or climbed the Kahukus: the tallest, the steepest, the meanest mountains there are if you're infantry, antelopes, mountain goats —anything. We were taught how to assault them, how to take basecamps, how to kill enemy: for Charlie was really made for war! We were mean! We were ugly! We never conceived of old people, men, women, children, babies: of Vietnamese being near us. Never did anyone tell us—

Oh no, I'm wrong. The day before we went to Vietnam, we were given an orientation talk, *Vietnam Our Host*. I should know: I had to give it (I also gave *Chemical, Biological, and Radiological Warfare*). The company made a horseshoe around me. I kept telling it, "Wake up! We're going to Vietnam! Wake up! Because it's our host—" Oh god, what a farce that was. I read off an SOP of "Do"s and "Don't"s that the Pentagon sent us. Items like—I don't remember. Do not insult the women. Do not *assault* the women. And—I'm too foggy about it. Items like "Be polite."

I had only three minutes for *Vietnam Our Host*. I did a very very poor job of it. I realize that now.

The next morning, at four o'clock all Charlie company was up and waiting to "Load up the buses, men!" We waited till one: we had pickets at Honolulu airport, and we didn't want to get stoned or struck by their STOP THE WAR signs. I've only guessed what the signs said: we snuck in another way, by Lua Lua Lei Ammunition Depot and Pearl Harbor.

We went to Vietnam on Pan American Airways. We

landed there on December 1, 1967, in—I didn't know, it could be Ojis, India, and I wouldn't know. I acted asinine that day. I almost thought, *It is hand-to-hand combat today,* and I stood in the trailer truck like the meanest, the most tremendous, the most dangerous weapon there is. My rifle slung low. My helmet pulled down. I even scowled! I realize now, I couldn't impress the Vietnamese less. None of them looked at me: *Another truck of GIs? Big deal,* and they couldn't give a rat's ass. I even saw a Vietnamese woman take a crap alongside us. But still I felt, *This is my day!* And these are my men! We're rough and we're tough, and Charlie's here: Charging Charlie! To end this damned war tomorrow!

We had been the best company in Hawaii. That was the Captain's doing: Captain Medina's. I really respect him. A man would have to commission close to a half million officers before he had someone equal to Captain Medina. A real leader: I think if Medina had gotten drunk and screwed every girl in Hawaii, the troops would have too. He had been strac, though: an outstanding soldier, and they tried to "soldier" too. He had the best platoons in Hawaii, and I would lead the first platoon in Vietnam. My sergeant would be Sergeant Cowen: a Negro, and a just beautiful individual. Gosh, I couldn't want a better platoon sergeant than him. I always told him, "Hell, Sergeant Cowen. You've been to Korea: I want a couple tips!" My squad sergeants would all be Negroes too: Sergeant Mitchell and Sergeant Bacon. I'm from the South, but I'm not a prejudiced person: I say the greatest people there are are Negroes. Mexicans such as Medina, Filipinos, Puerto Ricans, Italians, Poles: the greatest people there are. We had them all in Charlie company.

My best friend among the men was Specialist Weber. Now, there are GIs who keep bitching about the Army. But they still admire the GIs who say, "I'll try," and Weber was one. He was my RTO: my radio telephone operator and a platoon leader's dream. Say if I wanted to bullshit with the second platoon leader. Weber said, "Go to the bullshit push."

"The bullshit push?"

"Call him and say, 'Go to Jack Benny's Birthday.'"

"Jack Benny's—?"

"3900 kilocycles. Or the Spirit of St. Louis. At 2700 kilocycles. Or Outer Space—"

So that was us: Charlie company, and we were in Vietnam now. And seeing it through the open doors of a cattle car: a shanty land, the houses of cardboard and tin. I was awed: there seemed to be no nice sections anywhere. I felt superior there. I thought, *I'm the big American from across the sea. I'll sock it to these people here.*

We continued south. We took up residence inside our AO: our operations area, and met the Vietnamese people there. One thousand kids, out to solicit the laundry business when we had guard duty on a Vietnamese bridge. All the men loved them. Gave the kids candy, cookies, chewing gum, everything. Not me: I hated them. I had promised myself, *I'll act as if I'm never secure.* I hollered, I yelled, I threw rocks, I threw little kids in the river—yes! I was afraid of Vietnamese kids. At OCS, I had heard enough of kids putting things in a gasoline tank or a GI's hooch. I was afraid of prostitutes too (I'll come to the prostitutes later) but I was more afraid of Vietnamese kids: I had thousands there. I kept yelling, "Go or I throw you in water."

"You no do it, GI! Vietnamese bridge! I Vietnamese! I stay on bridge! Tonight, I bring all VC to bridge—" Oh, they would tantalize us. "I bring VC and they *cacadow* all American GI! I stay on bridge!"

"Okay, I throw you in."

"You number ten, GI! You number ten, GI! No throw me in—" I would throw him in. And listen to every kid say, "Oh, throw me in, GI!" They actually loved it.

This was a very strategic bridge for the AO. My orders were no Vietnamese there: the Colonel just wouldn't tolerate it. But the kids realized, *What can a GI do to us?* To spank them was an assault on a Vietnamese national, to scream—well, it couldn't hurt much. I could just tell the Colonel, "Sir, I'm throwing them off as fast as they're coming on." I had my ass chewed once by Captain Medina. I was taking a nap inside when my RTO said, "Ah—the Captain's outside, sir. He wants you." I went to Medina's jeep, "Yes sir?"

"Go back in. Get dressed." I had been disrespectful: nude, so I put a towel on.

"Yes sir. What is it?"

"Kids. All over the bridge."

"Sir, I can't keep them off day and—"

"Are you an officer of the United States Army?"

"Yes sir."

"And can you control your men?"

"Yes sir."

Which was a lie. Because the GIs just loved those kids, and I couldn't encourage them not to. I couldn't make the GIs believe, *They're bad. And they're going to harm us.* They really would help us so: shine shoes, do laundry, do everything. And promise us, "I friend." And sell us Coca-Cola. And teach us in Vietnamese, "I love you," "Where are the VC?" "Are you VC?" Those energetic kids! Everyone told me, "God, Lieutenant. Why try to stop it? Eighteen years and I never had anyone tell me, 'I friend.'"

But orders are orders. I said to Captain Medina, "Yes sir. I can control the men," and I went to a GI who loved kids: PFC Dursi. He always had a pack of the kids there, and I said, "I'm telling you now for the third time: I don't want kids here."

"I like kids, and I can't tell them, *Go away.*"

"It's that or you'll get an article fifteen." Or lose a PFC stripe.

"I don't give a good goddamn."

"All right. You've got an article fifteen."

I took him to Captain Medina: the Captain wouldn't put it in. He asked me, "Will it keep the kids away?"

"No, Dursi doesn't give a shit."

"Why should I do the paperwork?"

"And what do I do about those kids?"

"Well, you're a lieutenant, aren't you? And you can control your men?"

All right. I saluted him, he saluted me, Medina left and I went where the GIs were. "Someday," I said, "a little sonofabitch's going to grenade you." And left: I told myself, *Let them learn.*

The prostitutes too, I had orders on. Battalion said if the "boomboom girls" try to solicit us, I was to quickly shoo (I think that was it verbatim: shoo) the girls off, we shouldn't associate with the Vietnamese girls. A mother might hold the Army responsible or a congressman say, "He's giving his soldiers pussy. It isn't right." I told it to my platoon as I'd heard it. "You're members of the United States Army. And by the laws of the United States—" How did I phrase it? "Prostitution's illegal. And prostitutes come to this bridge at approximately 1800—"

"Yay! Bring on the prostitutes!"

"No one," I said, "is to prosper the prostitutes' business. Is that understood?"

It wasn't, of course. Face it: most every guy in America, the average guy is for pussy. To buy it, cheat it, steal it, get it however possible. What can the Army do? Announce? "There will be girls in. And they'll be starving. And they'll be telling you, 'My mother, my father, my sister, my brother is starving too.' And they'll be selling it, gentlemen, and if you touch it: article fifteen. Or a summary court." Say if you send every second man in your platoon to Leavenworth. You realize, *Gee, I have twenty people now. I'm going around at half strength now.* I say if a little pussy keeps a platoon together, a little pussy they've got.

At twilight, two of those boomboom girls came by. Dressed up and heavily made up for going to God-knows-where: the rouge on, the powder caked on, the "dink" or whatever the Vietnamese straw hats are on. One girl, one of her front two teeth wath mithing: she talked like thith. And looked stupefied, like a girl looking for the license plate of the truck that hit her, I don't know. A dumb-looking broad: the other was fairly flamboyant, though, and looked cute on a Honda fifty. A pimp in Italian shoes was driving it and telling guys, "Forty dollars."

The men acted natural about it. Cool, or what is the word? Blasé. As if, *They're extremely lucky if I sleep with them. I can have any girl in Asia*—but I could hear and I went outside. I said, "Sergeant, where are the bridge guards?"

"They're with the boomboom girls."

"Get them guarding the bridge," I said, and I broke the party up. "Men! You're a little horny now. But forty dollars—! Don't be damned fools." The pimp, it happened, was angry, anyhow: the troops had ridden his Honda around, and after getting it back again he left us. The boomboom girls too.

Pretty soon, up came three other motorbikes, six other boomboom girls, and their mamasan: madam. I was inside again but I heard the bidding. And bitching. And haggling. And everything, and I just couldn't take it. Remember: the Red Cross is great but not *that* great, the GIs are old enough to fight, to vote (or they should be) and make themselves money and spend it. And some would be dead in a month, so I went outside and I said, "Now Mamasan. You want twenty dollars. I have twenty soldiers. One dollar one GI."

"No no."

"One dollar every time."

"No no—" She compromised on $4 every man. All the girls all the night.

So there were who? Two girls in two of the bunkers—no, one girl in two of the bunkers. And two girls in *two* of the bunkers, right? And the mamasan—well, I had relieved a Negro lieutenant and he had briefed me. "She doesn't screw. Do you know, though? She is all right. She is twenty-eight. She stays here in the command bunker. Yours." All right, and I had invited the mamasan in. There were no chairs inside, only a pair of double-decker bunks made out of ammunition cans on PSP: the runway stuff. But being shy of a GI's bed, the mamasan sat on a Vietnamese mat on the bunker floor. She wore a Saigon: a long white gown, and a white pair of pants underneath it. Some paraffin in a C-ration can created sort of a chandelier to illuminate her. A very beautiful woman.

I said, "My name is Rusty."

She said, "My name—Susie."

I said, "Do you live around here?" I admit it, I'm shy about girls. I have to ask silly questions if I'm at a cocktail party back in Miami. "Do you live in Miami?" "Yeah." "Well gee. What part of Miami?" "The Shores." "Well gee. Do you work in Miami? Or do you always run to New York—" Stupid questions. Same as I asked of Susie in the command bunker then, but I didn't care: I would break the ice. Already, Susie had asked me to sit with her: I had jumped to it. I had thought, *It may be the first step.* I confess, I wanted to sleep with her.

Outside, I would hear the GIs get a little too rowdy, a little rambunctious. I would get up (I kept my RTO inside) and I would say, "We're still in Vietnam. We're not raising hell at Coney Island." Other times, I would see if the bridge guards were on. And once—I had said to Susie, "Cigarette?" I had them across on the ammunition crates, and I had started up. She being a Vietnamese she *jumped* up and right up into the C-ration paraffin can. It spilled, and Susie said, "*Ow—*" "*Oi—*" "*Oh—*" something in Vietnamese, and she hurried out. I followed her.

Susie was at the river: kneeling, letting her hair in, and rinsing the paraffin out. Or trying to, because, of course, it just became lumps, and Susie had to go back inside to try instead with a cheap plastic comb. Remember if you're at a swimming pool and a girl's putting suntan oil on? You go? You help rub it on? This combing gave me an in. Susie was a bit hesitant (in Vietnam a man doesn't comb a woman's hair), but I sat down and I began. I felt great compassion for Susie. I wished that I could kiss and caress her—if she would let me. Suddenly, one of her girls ran in saying a GI had hit her. Had popped her one. I asked the soldier, "Did you?"

"Hell no! She wouldn't screw for us."

"I do one time all GI! No do two times all GI!"

"Enough is enough," I told him.

"We want our twenty dollars then!"

"No no no no—"

At last, I think Susie told her, "You screw the GIs again." And when everyone left us, Susie leaned up against me. I put an arm around her, I smoked a Pall Mall and I was in bliss.

"Well—" my RTO told me. "I'm just about ready to go to sleep."

I said, "It's getting late."

He said, "It's awfully warm, I think. I'll sleep outside."

I said to Susie, "Sleep?"

She put her hands to her cheek in a praying position: sleep. She took an air mattress down (the other was on the floor already) and she lined it up. I got a poncho liner down, and I got another one for Susie. And we lay down together. And we made love.

And after that we talked. But oh—! To get an idea across took us hours, practically. Did you ever try to talk seriously with a girl whose vocabulary is "You GI," "You number one," "You number ten"? Or to pantomime a philosophy with a girl whose philosophy is opposite yours? Susie would say, "You no like VC. Why?" I would tell her the VC are bad, and Susie would say, "VC no hurt me, VC no hurt you." Or say, "You nice to VC, he nice to you." I would tell her the VC are bad for the Vietnamese people, and Susie would say, "Same same! VC Vietnamese. Vietnamese VC." All right: I would tell her the VC are communists and Susie would just say, *"No bitt,"* "I don't understand." She hadn't heard of communism or of democracy. What could I do about it? Tell her in a democracy the Vietnamese choose— no, I couldn't say it. What if she answered me, "I choose communism." Then what was I to do? Kill her? Or capture her? Or send her to a POW camp? If she's communist, that's what my duty was.

Sometimes, I sit down and cry now, I really do. For even in Roman times (in Roman movies) the Romans would talk to their enemies. As for me, I tried: I looked at those people, I looked in their eyes, I listened to their philosophies. And just couldn't counter them. I couldn't answer them. I was shut off as soon as someone said, *"No bitt."* I sat and I had a platoon there and I knew, *I can't talk to this man.* Or this woman. Or child (or a twelve-year-old in America even). I couldn't talk the language. I didn't know the customs. And yet—I had to convince a man that communism's bad. Or he would become a communist too: America's enemy, and god! Even the Good Book, the Bible, says, "You shall destroy your enemy." I just knew, *I must communicate with you. Or else you're dead.*

I gave $20 to Susie. I knew, *The party's over*, the prostitutes left and we got back to being soldiers again.

Or tried to. We did just everything wrong those days. We were new: we had a GI put a finger into a 45 once so the bullet wouldn't come out. On our first operation out, we even forgot the hand grenades. I ran to the ammo bunker: of course, the damn grenades had been crated so they could drop out of B-52s at ten thousand feet and it wouldn't bother them. I sat there, I got the crates apart, the individual cartons open, the adhesive tape off: it took considerable time and Medina just really chewed me. "Calley, I would relieve your ass in a goddamn second!" I felt humiliated: until my RTO told me, "Don't sweat it. I never met a man that didn't want to be late for war."

Our mission then was to blow up Vietnamese wells. Or try to: I think that a 500-pounder could do it, could anyhow make the water taste bad. But twenty pounds of TNT would make the well deeper, that's all. Our colonel, though, had a thing about wells: a bag about wells, and he wasn't about to tell a lieutenant why or listen to a lieutenant tell him, "Sir, you can't destroy wells with TNT. A bulldozer, maybe—"

"Lieutenant," the Colonel would say, "I'm very dissatisfied with you."

All right: so I put twenty pounds of TNT in, I threw that in, I didn't want to have singed eyebrows and I ran like hell. And *KABOOM*! It just rained, and the well would be full again. I bet all the GIs thought, *Oh, this is a fun-fun year*.

In fact, we didn't fire in anger all of December, 1967. There were no VC near us, probably. GIs before us had searched the AO and destroyed it and searched it and destroyed it. We just simulated. We practiced in the deserted hamlets. For instance: I saw a deserted house once, and I called my first artillery in. "Artillery, this is Charlie One. Request—ah, a fire mission."

"Roger. Send it."

"Grid—ah, 797557. Proximity of friendlies—ah, 400 meters. Azimuth—" I was new, and I was nervous about it.

"Roger. Will this be live artillery?"

"Yeah!"

"What will it be?"

"What have you got? Chocolate? Strawberry—" No, I didn't really say it.

"Will this be a battery one, battery two, battery three—"

"A battery six!"

"Stand by." A battery back at officer candidate school was a single gun. But in Vietnam—

Boomboomboomboom! And the world lit up: the house, the trees, the world was blowing away! It was a slow motion movie of some atomic bomb, and I knew everyone in America had heard it! President Johnson! Congress!

"Jesus," I said. "You're blowing away all of South Vietnam!"

"You wanted a battery six. You got it."

I learned more in December than in six months of manuals at OCS. One night, I took out an ambush party. All volunteers, since this was a mission many of us might die on: I really believed it. I was a dumb young second lieutenant, remember. I thought I'd slay—oh, a hundred VC by sunrise and I might end the war. So right after dark— No no, I didn't want to go after dark, and I got Medina to let us out during daylight hours. Even so, I couldn't find an ambush area like any I'd seen at OCS. Old empty cornfields were all I saw. No bushes, no trees, no place to camouflage ourselves: I looked over *hell*, and I had to put that ambush in a cornfield after dark.

It kept going crunch: I crawled around, I placed each man, I told him, "Be quiet," but I made hordes of noise in that cornfield stuff. I dropped my rifle once and I couldn't find it. I realized, *God, I'm spooking the water buffalos, and I'll have herds overrunning me. I'm waking the VC nation up.* They always said at OCS, the thing with an ambush was to keep perfectly quiet. To tie up things so they wouldn't rattle. Not to use rifle slings. To carry a full canteen so the water wouldn't slosh (I didn't think of asking them, "How can I drink? It won't be full anymore.") But tonight, if there were VC within miles of us I bet they laughed themselves to death.

Well, I hadn't been in Vietnam long. I told every man, "Stay awake! They will be here pretty soon," and I patted everyone's back. I knew the VC were nearby because—well, I was in South Vietnam. There was a war going on. There must be VC or the people, the President, the congress, the generals wouldn't fly me here, would they? To lie here to look at a road nobody's coming on? Our captain: Medina wouldn't send me anywhere if I couldn't get a big kill count, right? He knew his poop, and I was excited, I was tensed up, I was kill crazy there. And suddenly clump! I said, *They're coming*.

"Lieutenant?" Just the machine gunner with me. "Lieutenant? Where are you?"

"I'm over here."

"Where?"

"I'm over here."

"Sir, can I load the machine gun now?"

Oh god. I had been taught at OCS to wait until now to load it: a safety rule. "Oh yeah! Load the machine gun."

"I'll do it, Lieutenant."

Now, does anyone know how an M-60 sounds if you're loading it? How those cartridges sound? A *clink clink clink*. Then a *clank clank clank*. Then the horrible sound of the bolt closing, *CLANK*. I lay there and I just cringed! I said, *God, they never said it was this way at OCS*. Never, the

hardest thing in Vietnam is silence. Why, a guy on this ambush started to *scream* at us, "Waaa! Motherfucking son-
ofa—" You know, the whole routine. A regular tantrum. I
couldn't tell if VC were stabbing him or were doing what,
but I ran towards him. I got hit, incidentally, by his fatigue
shirt, the GI was standing and screaming and stripping
wildly. Was doing a maniac strip.

I said, "Kid, what's the problem?"

He said, "These goddamn ants!"

I said, "What goddamn ants? Where?"

He said, "Everywhere! On me!"

I said, "God."

I relocated him, and I settled down. Ten o'clock. Eleven
o'clock. Midnight: and I got disappointed, I got annoyed.
Never at OCS had we waited three hours, at OCS we were
stumbled on promptly. I really began to despise the VC
then. Not only are VC communists but they're overdue,
damn it: they won't hurry into my killing zone. I thought I
might call up Captain Medina, "Charlie Six? This is Charlie
One. I think I've made an error, sir. I've waited three hours,
and the VC haven't shown." I was depressed, until it began
to register that we had caused so much noise that—*the VC
must know I'm here. And are sneaking up.* And then I was
terror struck, and I grabbed for the radio. A choice was to
call up Medina and say, "Sir, I think the enemy blew it. I'm
coming in." I thought of a second choice as I grabbed it: I
said, "Charlie Four! Charlie Four!" The mortar platoon.
"This is Charlie One."

"Roger, Charlie One. What you got?"

"I got a fire mission! Continuous illumination!"

"Roger, Charlie One."

From then on, I had continuous flares over me. High yellow flares, and I saw for miles around (of course everyone for miles around could also see me). I had those flares for, I guess ninety minutes until—

"Charlie One. This is Charlie Six." It was Captain Medina.

"Ah—Charlie Six? This is Charlie One."

"Charlie One. Now what in the goddamn hell?"

"Charlie Six. It's a dark and rainy night and—"

"You nitwit! You're without a doubt the most stupid second lieutenant on the face of this earth."

"Yes sir. I know sir. I'm stupid sir. What should I do?"

"Turn off them goddamn lights!" And then to the mortar platoon, "Charlie Four? Did you roger that?"

"Roger."

And four hours later, the sun rose. The night was a comedy of errors, but it didn't matter much: we weren't dead, we had lived and learned. We soon forgot about those wells. Soon if I called artillery in, I didn't say, "Grid—" "Proximity—" "Azimuth—" I said, "I may have an SHIT," a Sniper Hidden In a Tree. "I want artillery. Savvy?" And they would answer me, "Roger!" The next time I took an ambush out, I could do it.

But there the depression set in. After my second, my third, my fourth, my fifth, my tenth, my twelfth, my twentieth—ambush, I still hadn't had a VC in my killing zone, and I had had perfect ambush sites, too. I thought, *What am I pulling ambushes for?* I hadn't met any VC in the daylight either. What am I running patrols for? Or looking for? Or humping for? What did I have sixteen months of training for? Now, Charlie was made for killing! Charlie was made for war! Charlie was combat infantry: *We want to kill!*

Not half as much as our colonel did. He kept asking us, "Any body count?"

"No sir."

"No body count?"

"Nobody there to shoot at."

"You better get on the stick sometime."

"Yes sir."

It got so, I cringed if I ever heard helicopter blades. Our colonel would look for VC suspects from—oh, ten thousand feet, and play platoon leader with us. "Oh, Charlie One? I spotted a VC suspect. A few minutes from you." Of course, the Colonel could go a kilometer in thirty seconds and I was in the damn foliage: it might take me a lifetime. "Go where the purple smoke is, Charlie One." Of course, there was a fifty-meter hill in between us.

"Negative on the purple smoke."

"You don't see it? Sonofabitch, I'll throw another purple smoke."

"Negative on the purple smoke."

"You sonofabitch! It's right on the other side of the little hill!"

I got just a little fed up. He had that goddamn chopper there, he should land it and capture the VC suspect himself. Or shoot him: I had to walk there, as if I couldn't be ambushed at that purple smoke.

"Get the VC, Charlie One?"

"Yeah."

"Get any body count?"

"No. It's just an old lady taking her taxes in." Or a little boy, or a little girl, or it might be a farmer there with a wooden hoe. I would radio, "He seems friendly."

"Oh does he? He has that goddamn corral there. What is it?"

"You said it: a goddamn corral. He seems proud of it."

"Destroy it."

"You want to destroy it? All right," I would say, and I would tear the corral apart, get all the wood together, get a hot fire going—

"You didn't get a body count?"

"No—"

"You better start doing the job, Lieutenant, or I'll find someone who can."

I thought, *Oh, screw you, Colonel. What do you really want of me? Shoot him? If all you can think of is Kill them.*

Kill—the war's never over. You stay there another day and you can kill someone else. And someone *else*. Or do you kill everyone in South Vietnam? And say, "We have won, we are going home." I imagine so: just everything in today's society is "How many thousands?" "How many millions?" "How many billions?" And everything was in Vietnam: was numbers, and I had to furnish them. So television could say, "We killed another thousand today," and Americans say, "Our country's great."

The body count—damn. I did what every lieutenant had to: I finally got us a body count. I mean I reported it. One night I said, "We have incoming, sergeant."

"Sir?"

"We have incoming rounds."

"I see." He went where the GIs were, and *tatatata*: he started shooting it up. Artillery guns, machine guns, we had a mock little firefight, and I called in a body count: three, and a combat loss of some compasses. It was near inventory time, and I had lost those compasses somehow.

It was getting ridiculous there. I couldn't keep the GIs awake now. In one platoon, the GIs went without helmets on: a T-shirt and shower shoes on. I had troops without iodine pills, or they would open the claymore mines and use the C-4 explosive for cooking fuel: for cooking the C-rations over. I'd see a GI with an empty mine and say, "Listen, dummy. It won't make a loud enough noise now. It won't scare the enemy now, and we definitely do want to scare him."

"Yeah, do I get another one?"

"Well, do you leave the explosive in?"

"Yeah—if I get the heat tablets, too."

It was getting ridiculous! Once, I had a GI with a grenade launcher: sort of a one-gauge shotgun. He shot every grenade off so he wouldn't have to patrol with us. And once, a GI woke up in a grouchy mood: he had been standing guard, I guess, and he had fifteen minutes' sleep. And someone told him, "Okay. We are moving out." He may have thought, *I can't take it*, I don't know: or was constipated, but he just picked up his rifle and he threw the thing away. I understood why: it happens that way in civilian life, too. An auto mechanic, he throws a monkey wrench down. An executive throws a pencil down, and a cleaning woman her mop. But people get in a mood, and it builds and it builds.

On patrols, the GIs didn't talk to each other much. A man might say, "I got a letter today. My girl is screwing everyone in Atlanta." Or a GI might tell me, "Aw shit. I don't want to carry this."

"Aw shit. I don't want to hear your shit," I would say.

"Why do I have to carry an empty can?"

I didn't know. I didn't know why a cheap plastic water can is a nonexpendable item. I didn't know why a GI pays ninety-eight cents for losing one. Or why we were on this damn patrol, and I didn't want the GIs asking me. Imagine if I answered honestly—

"Why are we doing it?"

"Because the Captain said so."

"Why did the Captain say so?"

"I didn't ask."

"It's a simple question, isn't it? Why didn't you ask?"

"Because the Captain would tell me, 'Because the Colonel said so.' And then I would probably ask him, 'Why did the Colonel say so?' "

"Why did the Colonel say so?"

"Because the General told him, 'I've nothing better to do.' "

"If they've nothing better to do, Lieutenant—why are we in Vietnam?"

Seriously. OCS always told us, GIs will think you're a dumb damned officer if you can't answer them, and I knew, *I can't.* I couldn't bring the GIs' spirits up: I wondered too, *Now where in the goddamn hell are the VC here? Or aren't there any?*

And one day, Medina assembled us. He said we were moving north that day: to another AO. He told us, "There will be action now," he said it and raised our morale. When the convoy left, the GIs were laughing and throwing the kids their rations and whistling and yelling at Vietnamese girls, "Boomboom!" I sat up front thinking, *I'll see the enemy now. I'll get a body count:* I was pleased. We went a hundred kilometers, and we established camp on a steep-sided hill: we called it Uptight. It reminded me, sometimes, of a sinking ship, it seemed that a thousand rats deserted it whenever the VC mortars hit us. Rats running out of every-where: the tents, the trenches, the rats stepping right on the mines, sometimes, and blowing up. But we weren't aware of the rats except then. It was pretty on Uptight: we could look at a hundred paddies and, a little beyond them, at the China sea. At water buffalos and at fishing boats, too.

We were in a task force now. Its mission would be a VC battalion in a big fishing village: the village of Mylai One. We got orders, and I said to Captain Medina, "I'm ready to go." Our company climbed off of Uptight, and we attacked in February, 1968.

And failed. We didn't get within two kilometers of Mylai One. As soon as the farmers saw us, they became animals: antelopes, and they really loped away. I knew, *The farmers know*, and sure enough there was a *click click click* from the other side of the river. I was pinned down by VC rifle fire, and I answered it with every artillery there is: VT and HE and WP or "Willie Peter" shells, and with the Guns A Gogo. Do you know about those? A couple of Army helicopters played the Air Force. I just popped smoke and I called them, "I'm on the smoky side, the enemy's on the other side. Go give 'em hell."

"Roger!"

And two Chinooks went in with rockets and minigun rounds, and as they banked around they had a quad fifty or four fifty-caliber machine guns on the tailgate: that was the

Guns A Gogo. I thought, *This is the world's greatest thing*, but no. All that stress: it tore the Chinooks in half, almost. It was another great idea, but it didn't work out.

Anyhow, we crawled from the riverside under the Guns A Gogo. Charlie (the VC rifleman) waited till we were out on a levee, and he zapped us again. He really slapped it to us! I called the artillery unit on Uptight, "I've got a target!"

"What will it be?" Meaning what gun.

"Goddamn it, I don't care! As long as there's lots of it!"

"Roger!"

I used up every artillery shell on Uptight that day. Everything but the flechette rounds or "shotgun shells" that the artillery uses if VC are overrunning it. I used up one million dollars of artillery shells that day. It's funny: how many times do people ask, "If you had a million dollars how would you spend it?" I have to answer now, "I've already spent it. I've burned up a million dollars of ammunition." I realize, I'm back in America now and money, money, money, is so important now. "God," people say. "There were two VC shooting at him, so this nutty lieutenant burned up a million dollars. God." I didn't give a damn, though: it didn't bother me. I had troops getting shot at. If it took fifty million dollars of artillery to save a PFC's life, I'd have poured it on. I'd have dropped a hydrogen bomb if I'd had it!

Because: one million dollars didn't do. A rifle shot got my RTO on his radio harness, it shattered and it tore his kidney out. He rolled off the levee saying to me, "I been shot."

I screamed for the medic. "Doc!"

"What's wrong?"

"Get over here! Weber's been hit!"

"How bad is he?"

"Get the hell over here! He's dying!"

Weber: everyone loved him. He had written to home often, I knew. And there was a Swedish girl, a student, there: a doll, supposedly, and he had dreamt of going home and meeting her. And—

"Charlie Six. This is Charlie One."

"Charlie One?"

"I got an elephant here." A dead man.

"The hell you do. Stop fucking around and—"

"I'm not fucking around here. I got an elephant here."

"Okay, sweetheart—"

It must sound horrible: *sweetheart*. But you can't hear the inflection in Medina's voice: the vibration there. He was about to cry himself, and he just forced himself to say it.

"Okay, sweetheart! And keep fucking around, and you'll get the others killed too!"

It was true. I was ready to sit around and to sob about my RTO: I had to keep control here, or I'd lose what's left. It was as if Medina said, "It isn't for a sweetheart here. The people of America didn't say be a sweetheart here. They said be a sonofabitch and win the war." All right: I got professional about it. I called a medical helicopter in: a Dustoff. I told it, "You're coming here for a quartermaster case. If you don't think you'll make it—" I admit it: I would leave him, so as to not jeopardize the chopper crew. But they hovered over, and we lifted him on: a horrible job.

It had the GIs shook up. One soldier told me, "I never knew a dead person before. I was going to Weber's for Christmas, and I just realized, *He won't be there. Or anywhere—*" And some soldiers blamed it on me: I read this a while ago in Seymour Hersh's *My Lai 4*. It says, the GIs were calling it Calley's stupidity that we had just walked on the levee, rather than in the river near it. I admit it: I was stupid that day. But what if I'd walked in the river and it had mines inside it? What if a VC guerilla had a machine gun on it? *A beautiful ambush site*, I had thought. *A river that is just shoulder high, and all the GIs in it.* I like a fool walked on the levee instead, and Weber got hit.

Got killed. The first one in Charlie company killed, and I had another go into shock because of it. Or because of the incoming fire, or because of the cold and wet: I didn't know, but he became like a Zombie. We had to coach him all the way out, "We're getting out. We're going home." To hold his hand, practically, as we crawled two hundred meters to Mylai Three. It had been bombed out, of course, but a mamasan there had a fire going. Or rather I told her, "We want a fire," and she began stacking wood for us. In her fireplace there was a hot coal, still: the mamasan took a dry reed to it, blew on it, and touched a few little twigs with it. When there was a fire on, I told her, "*Get out,*" and I put the Zombie near it, shaking and shivering. I slapped him a little: nothing, no reflex whatsoever. I took my C's and brewed up some coffee for him. I slapped him a little harder, and I heard him say, "Don't hit me." He had come around, but he just couldn't forget, *Weber*—

I found us some motor oil for the machine guns: we didn't have a gun that hadn't jammed. I kept telling the troops, "Dig in," "Do this," "Do that," so they wouldn't go into shock themselves, but I didn't want to stay overnight in Mylai Three. A village is the last damned place to RON: to remain overnight in. There would be Vietnamese all around us. Old mamasan might come with an AK-47 to show us whose hooch we were really in, a VC battalion behind her. I called to Captain Medina, "It's shaggy here."

"And—?"

"I'd rather haul ass for Uptight."

"Roger. We'll haul ass too."

So that was our first assault on Mylai One. At Uptight, I threw down my combat gear in Weber's bunker: mine, and I tried to start on the after-action report.

Coordinates 722805. Flat fertile area. Medium population. Moved out in column formation. Went—

And that's when the artillery people came in. With a couple of six-packs of Ballantine's.

"Aren't you Charlie One?"

"Yeah."

"You sure did a lot of shooting there!"

"Yeah."

"We ran completely out of ammo at four o'clock—"

"Yeah. You were great today."

"We figured it up. We expended a million dollars' worth of ammo. We were getting into the eight-inch rounds, and boy! They're expensive!"

"Yeah."

I like the artillery people. All year they're on a hill pulling a damn lanyard: *bang, bang, bang,* and they never get to see anything blow up. I like if I can encourage them and say, "Outstanding." Or even, "Chalk up a body count of twelve." It helps the artillery's morale: but I couldn't do it. I hadn't seen a VC all that day. I knew damn well, *Weber's dead. A boy in the second platoon has no legs anymore. A boy in the third platoon—*

I had to do it. I wrote in the after-action report, "VC body count six."

Medina was a tremendous officer. The next day, he had us digging ditches and building bunkers: everything except sit on our asses thinking of Weber and thinking, *Gee. I may be the next to go.* He didn't call us together until late.

He told us what happened at Mylai One. He said, Alpha company had landed west of it: Alpha was the assault force that day. It had been fired on from behind, though, from the village of Mylai Six. It took heavy casualties, and Bravo company had landed south and had gotten tangled in a minefield there. It took heavy casualties too. Our company, Charlie company, had gone north, and we had been lucky: we lost only one GI. Medina said, "The way not to lose more men is bring the old punch back, is bring the morale back up. Is unite." We had a memorial service for Weber, and we went to building bunkers again. At last the troops understood it, *Some people here, if they get a chance they'll kill us.*

If only we could discover who! At seven each day, we would start out through the villages to reconnoiter them: and as Weber was, we were sniped at. We never learned who by, though. Of the infantry's mission here, we didn't get to part one: to *find*, to close with, and to destroy the VC. We never knew who the snipers were, and the Vietnamese told us, "We don't know, either." It frustrated us. It hurt our morale. My soldiers said, *God, am I dreaming? Or going mad?* We had been in Vietnam three months: we were losing men, we were being nickel-and-dimed away, we were being picked off. We were in Vietnamese villages daily, and we still hadn't seen one VC—

I'll correct that. We saw a VC sniper once: he fired a few rounds and he beat it. We chased him to a village, and he was still panting when we caught him: caught him in bed, incredibly. He tapped on his chest as though telling us, "I have heart disease and I'm always panting. I'm always in bed these days." Of course, it *might* be another man. I was quite sure, *It's him, I've caught the VC*, but I couldn't prove it. His rifle, we had already seen a woman running out of the village with it. He carried an ID card, and we couldn't call him a VC unless he confessed it. All right: we carried a rope to set every booby trap off, to climb up a tree, to come off a cliff, to get people out of a well and to put people into a well to wash themselves: whatever. It was something else to tote around endlessly, and I had a GI tie a hangman's noose in it. I threw it over a tree matter-of-factly, and I told the Vietnamese, "You shoot at GI. You *cacadow*." He knew that I meant, "You're dead," but he wasn't scared and he wouldn't say, "I did it." I felt, if I sent him to the task force and if they tortured him, he still wouldn't admit it. What could we do? It was bad for the GI morale, but I freed him.

He was about forty-five. I've heard people say, "He is past military age." I say that's hogwash: at forty-five, an American would be paraplegic or without any gumption who doesn't think that he can defend his wife, his children, and his family. It was hard finding the VC there because anyone could be a VC. Someone of seventy-five, if he couldn't shoot he could act as S-2 or intelligence officer. He could tell the VC where the company was or how many minutes it took us to get back to Uptight. To show the VC where the trail was, he could tie a cloth to the bushes beside it. Or he could act as S-4 or supply officer: supply the VC with their rice and their cooking oil. I think I had heard in grade school that an army marches on its stomach. Was it Napoleon said it? He'd have controlled the world if he hadn't lost his logistics line to Russia and his troops hadn't starved. A soldier moves on logistics, and a VC food-supply officer was as deadly as a VC shooting a rifle at us. And damn harder for us to identify.

Even a child could be a VC there, exactly as OCS told us. A soldier is walking along, say. He's hellishly hot. He's irritated. His bandolier: his ammunition is getting hung up on the goddamn bushes, and he is saying, *It's eating my shoulders away. I've got to get rid of it.* "Ahhhhh," and he throws the damn thing away and he charges on. Along come the little kids, and they carry the bandolier off for the VC to shoot at that soldier with. Or say we break camp: the kids come in and they canvass it for an empty ration can. A bandolier and a ration can, a kid could make a grenade from. And throw it: I had to go through the villages thinking, *Which are the VC kids?*

It frustrated us. Intelligence didn't tell us, "Joe is a VC guerilla." It didn't give us a list of VC addresses: Intelligence didn't know, and the Army didn't give us a lie detector, either. Or a paraffin kit: if it ever did, a GI would use it for keeping candy bars in, I'm sure. So every day, I went where the snipers were and I said, "Where are the VC?" And people would tell me, "We don't know," or they would gesture to me, "We like the GIs here. We wouldn't shoot you." At times, I would cordon the village off to search for a rifle: nothing. I would leave, and a minute later we would be sniped at again—damn! It was hard getting the GIs to think that we could accomplish things here. My men asked me, "Where are we going next?"

"To 711833."

"Why are we going there?"

I couldn't answer that. I didn't know why the Colonel sent us to those coordinates. I didn't have the S-2 intelligence reports. I was a second lieutenant, and I was there in a vacuum: in a jar. If someone took off the lid, I went where he said without knowing why. If a GI ever asked *me*, I just joked about it. "I know we aren't going to have medals pinned on. I know there won't be a band there and a big parade. I know extremely well, we won't have a Roman orgy there—"

"Why are we going there?"

"I'll know after we get there. Is that a good answer, troop?"

It wasn't. The troops didn't know why we didn't stay on Uptight or in Hawaii. "All of this walking, all it causes is casualties, sir." I got so I stayed away from them. I went through my chain of command: my sergeants, and I would communicate through them. I liked the Army sergeants: the professionals, who just didn't question the United States Army and the United States. But the young privates—well, if I even stopped for a C-ration lunch with one he would ask me, "Why are we in Vietnam, sir?"

"We are here to stop communism. If we don't, it will conquer all of Vietnam, Cambodia, Thailand—"

"But sir. How is this getting shot at stopping communism? We still haven't seen a VC."

"Write to your congressman, damn it! I didn't draft you."

I couldn't talk to the soldiers under me: I was a very in-adequate leader, I think. I was criticized for it in Hersh's book. It says there, it is amazing that the Army had thought me officer material. It quotes the troops,

> He was one of those guys they take off the street.
> I wondered how he got through OCS.
> It was kind of hard to show respect for him.
> He was always doing things wrong. Never right.
> He didn't know what was going on.

And they're right. And they're perfectly right. At officer candidate school (if they didn't bullshit me) I knew what was going on, but didn't know now. I didn't know why in the goddamn hell we were in Vietnam. Or even know who to ask about it. Captain Medina? Medina didn't know it. Colonel Barker? General Koster? President Johnson? I couldn't give the GIs answers, and the GIs all thought of me, *Shmuck*. I wish I had known how to bullshit with them. It's a leadership trait, and the second platoon leader had it: Lieutenant Brooks. I admired him. He could con the GIs into talking of drag races: anything else. Of good racing times, or could go and play cards with the GIs, win their money, and say, "We are moving out." To get a job done without dissension: that was a very happy trait of Lieutenant Brooks's. A knack.

I didn't have it. I couldn't shoot the shit, myself. I couldn't tell the GIs anything but, "We are moving out."

"Why?"

"On account of I say so. Is that a good enough answer, troop?"

"Aw—"

I did as OCS taught me. I didn't say, "I'm the boss around here," but I let the GIs think it. I knew, *I am one little pea in a peapod. And they're churning us up into peasoup*, but I didn't say it. I had this thing, and I didn't drop it. I acted big: I tried to let everyone think, *We accomplish things here*. I tried to keep up the esprit de corps.

I didn't. I let those doubts show, and the GIs saw through me: I read it in Hersh. They said, "Who is Calley kidding?"

> He made something out of himself he wasn't.
> He reminded me of a kid trying to play war.
> Everyone used to joke about him.

I was a phoney: true. The best thing might be if I had been honest, I think—but no. I couldn't go around like a piss ant if I was to keep their morale up. I couldn't say, "I don't know what I'm doing here. I think I'm screwed up. And the Army's screwed up. But men: tomorrow we go to Mylai One. *And kill those sonofabitches*—" I couldn't say it, I couldn't think it! What do I do if America's really screwed up? Defect?

I wasn't about to. I believe in America, and I wouldn't be disloyal to it. I wouldn't say, "Captain Medina, I'm sorry. You've only got two platoons."

"No, I've got three platoons. I've got the first platoon, the second—"

"I'm sorry. The first platoon has just walked off." Certainly not, I wouldn't throw down my rifle and say, "I quit," or demoralize the GIs just because of beliefs. In Vietnam, I wore a large face and I tried to keep people's spirits up: I did what every officer ought to. Read about the Pentagon in *The Limits of Intervention*, by Townsend Hoopes. Isn't it what those undersecretaries did? And Robert McNamara?

Something new: we went to a Vietnamese village where the GI morale went *up*. Someone there had been shooting us with mortar shells even, but, of course, when we got there everyone was an old papasan, an old mamasan, or a child saying, "We love the GIs." Everyone was friendly until we started to turn up VC flags. I realized then, *We were being taunted. We were being made a mockery of.* And damn it: when we moved out of this village and we were a hundred meters from it, they again socked it to us. Medina phoned, and he got province permission to go to that village to burn it. That's what the GIs wanted: to burn it! They held up their matches and Zippos, and they burned the hooches down. The people looked shocked, as though telling us, "Gee, you're burning our houses down." And they picked up and left us. They didn't patronize us. They knew the GIs meant business now.

Myself, I got a few "rest and recuperation" days at a sea resort, at Vungtau, Vietnam. The seashore wasn't on limits, though. It was February, 1968: the Tet offensive, the VC were on the warpath in Vungtau as everywhere else, and I couldn't leave the President hotel. I went to the hotel restaurant: closed. The bar was closed too. In that dreadful heat the Turkish bath was open, though, and I went downstairs for one. I tried, but I couldn't get a "special" from the cute little masseuse there. She recommended a teahouse down the street, but it wasn't on limits because of Tet. Upstairs again, and I played with the room light switch: it just fascinated me. Just think of telling them all in Mylai Three, "I touch and a light comes on." They wouldn't understand me! I flushed the toilet twice, I took a shower again, I figured, *Well, what the hell*, and I walked down to the hotel's front door. I asked the MP how the teahouse was.

"It's fine—"

I nodded, and I bolted off. I had just three days in Vungtau for a last fling before dying: I really thought so. I thought, *If there's anything that I want to do, I'll do it*. I ran across into the teahouse but I stayed safe: I got a haircut there so I'd be sitting there if the MPs came after me. They didn't, and I went farther into the teahouse.

A typical oriental one. Only there was an RCA color television console there in Early American Style: I guess they

got it through the PX, somehow. At home it would sell for
$600 easy. It was gorgeous, but it wasn't on because things
were so slow during the Tet offensive. In a liquor chest there
was Silver Fox, Canadian Club, Tiger Beer, and Jack Daniel's, and I asked them for a Daniel's. I didn't take the home-
rolled cigarettes, though. I can't really say, "It's illegal," if I
am off limits myself and I'm there to prosper a prostitute,
but I am against marijuana. I don't frequent with it.

I sat sipping the Daniel's. Straight (in Vietnam, ice is non-
potable) and I sat saying niceties with the mamasan there.
"It's a nice day." "And you've a nice house." "And you're a
nice man. I like you." At last, the mamasan went to the
phonograph part of the console to put on—I don't really
know, I don't know the Cream from the Electric Prunes. To
put an American record on. A very attractive girl of French
and Vietnamese origin came in, and Mamasan told me,
"This is Yvonne."

I said, "How are you?"

Yvonne said, "I fine."

"Do you like her?"

"I do."

"She dances—"

"*No no.*"

"I don't really care to dance either, please."

"She gives back rubs."

"I maybe buy back rub."

"You maybe buy more?"

"How much is more?"

"I like you. Fifteen hundred piasters for back rub and more."

Only fifteen dollars. A deal, and we went upstairs and we stayed there all day. In general, there is no worse—partner, or whatever, than a Vietnamese girl. GIs think that a Vietnamese girl is a substitute for sex. It beats beating off—no, I wouldn't even say so. Yvonne though, I had something inside me that badly wanted to love her, and I made an effort to. I enjoyed her extremely. I have her picture still: a rounded face, thirty-two twenty-two thirty, a pretty bust, a pretty girl. And smart too! Yvonne knew the population of Paris and practically every city in France. And how far apart in kilometers every city was. She always beat me at USA capitals too. She asked me, "Kansas."

"I don't know."

"Topeka! Washington."

"Olympia." I knew that one, I had taken training at Fort Lewis, Washington.

"Georgia— Get under the bed! I don't know who it is," Yvonne would tell me: Yvonne scared the living hell out of me when anyone knocked. Was it American MPs? Was it VCs? In fact, we were raided later, but it meanwhile was Calley under the bed and Yvonne at the door talking to I don't know who. She really cared about me. She protected me.

She meant a lot to me. Damn, do you know why Yvonne was a prostitute? It's very sad. I could pay her $10,000 and she would send it, every cent, to her mother, that's how the Vietnamese are. And she would pick up a GI an hour later. I even asked her: if I gave her a million dollars what? "I go, I take care of my mother." Which is a beautiful thing, I believe, but god! Her mother once was a prostitute for the French, and Yvonne having come of age is a prostitute too. A good kick for a GI: sure, but a woman ought to have something more. A husband. A family. To drive to the suburbs every day: I don't know, but I say there's something more and Yvonne was just cheated of it. I wanted to seize her and say, "Jesus Christ! Believe me! It isn't life! It isn't the way the world is! Let's steal away to America! I'll show you!" A daydream, but I was in Vietnam to help these people, right? I'd love to have swept her to Miami, my family's home. See the shows and tell her, "You're free now. We'll go to the Castaways, the Carillon, the Boomboom Room, the Fontainebleau. Tomorrow we'll go to La Gorce Country Club—"

No no. It wouldn't work. She wouldn't be welcome in Miami ever. The money society, the ones playing golf at La Gorce: if I took her, Yvonne wouldn't be accepted there. Then say if I took her to the middle class. She still wouldn't be accepted there. The average guy in Miami, he doesn't accept the Jews, he doesn't accept the Negroes, he doesn't accept any but Christian and Caucasian. Put in a Mongol there, and what would she be? A Mongol. Not a human being. Americans all say, "Gee. We want to help those people. As long as they don't move in—" And then Americans scorn them. I had a cousin once. He tried to get married to a Korean girl, and I mean it: his mother was in a tizzy. And there were the tourist ladies at a restaurant table in Bangkok once. Old horny bats, all of them watching the Thais sitting with us and whispering, "I think it's revolting." Till a lieutenant with us interrupted them, "Excuse me, I know we are mixing races here. But the girl you're calling a whore is the prime minister's daughter. She understands every word, and you're making a bad impression upon the Thais."

In fact, the girl was a whore. Sure: but Yvonne was one too. And a hell of a lot better person than some I see at Miami Beach. Ask anyone back in Miami what he would use a million dollars for. He may say, "A yacht," he won't say, "To care for my mother and father." Yvonne will, or Yvonne will say, "To keep learning things." The damn population of Paris! As fluent in French as in Vietnamese! Now, this was a prostitute? This was a lowlife whore? I was there in a Vietnamese teahouse and I was thinking, *Gee, I'm great. I'm American*: I got a flushing toilet and an electric light that I can switch on. I am needed here. I was sitting there and I suddenly saw, *She's speaking to me in English.* Most of the trouble today is communication. We can't communicate with the Russians, we can't communicate with the Negroes, we can't communicate with the twelve-year-olds: but Yvonne can communicate with us. So who is smarter than who? Or who needs who? I bet, if I asked her to Miami she would tell me, "I like my village, thank you. I

don't like the Fontainebleau. I don't really want the American Dream—"

I don't want to think about it. Jesus, I would be some officer if I let myself think, *I can't help the Vietnamese people.*
I was on leave, anyway, and I didn't want to be depressed. I
didn't want to go into heavy philosophy. I escaped it: I had
a Daniel's, hot towels, etcetera, and I conked. When the
raiders came, it wasn't the VC but the Vietnamese police:
the white mice, as GIs say, and I wasn't under the bed now.
I had become tired of it. I had been defenseless there, and I
was just having a Daniel's when the white mice hit us. I ran
straight out. It was past curfew, and if I was shot there
would be no questions asked. A day earlier, a few mamasans
had gone right into a Thompson submachine gun: I saw
them killed, and I ran thinking, *God, I could be running the
levee outside of Mylai Three.* I ran catty-corner into the
President hotel, and I packed. I kept thinking of Charlie
company: combat. I didn't think of Yvonne again. Ours was
a superficial thing, that's all. A wartime romance.

I caught an early airport bus. I
helped to clean up the bodies from a VC rocket attack, and
I continued to Uptight. People up there were in a panic, almost. The choppers were in with bundles of blood-covered
clothes: the worst were a couple of blood-covered boots

with a GI's feet inside them. The pilot said, "Charlie company's in a minefield now."

It had to happen sometime! God, a guy couldn't go where there wasn't a minefield here. The whole side of Uptight was a minefield, and a whole monastery here was a minefield too. On our minefield maps, the Army had drawn in blue circles for friendly minefields and red circles for VC minefields and yellow circles for suspected minefields: there were a million circles! That we had been walking in ninety percent of February and playing at Russian roulette with. I would say to Medina, "God. Are we going in *there*? It's a minefield," but the Captain went or the enemy would sit in its minefield forever. Or would dig up the damn things to use somewhere else. We once caught a VC ten years old in a Vietnamese army minefield that he had been digging up. In his little bag he had four mines: the fifth had blown up, though, the whole right side of his face had blown off. Of course, we called a helicopter in. Another time, we saw in some paddies lots of bouncing betties with a straw in the safety holes. And knew, *A farmer is relocating them. It's rice-planting time.* In fact, so many people relocated mines that the Army said, "We don't know anymore where the minefields are." A unit could be far outside of the colored circles, and it would see a bouncing betty pop up. And tear about thirty holes in a GI's belly. Cut him in half.

It was happening now to Charlie company. "A cry started going up, *Medic*," Medina would say as a witness at Fort Benning, Georgia. "I took the medic to where the individual was. He was split from his crotch to his chest: I've never seen anything so unreal. The intestines, the liver, the stomach looked just like plastic. The medic started to pick him up, I reached under his arms, and we set him on top of another mine: I fell backwards. The medic was starting to go to pieces on me. He looked as if he had stood behind a screen, and somebody had taken paint and splattered it through. He had blood all over him. I grabbed him, I shook him, I said, 'My god! Don't go to pieces on me,' I hit him, I slapped him, I knocked him. I helped him up, I seen on his religious medal a piece of liver, I tried to get it off—"

I knew the dead soldier. You couldn't be gloomy around him, he enjoyed himself so. That boy, I say is as innocent as any baby in Mylai Four. I thought, *God, I'm like a deserter here.* I kept throwing the clothes from the helicopter, and I thought, *I've been screwing off, I've been running out: I have to get in to Charlie company.* I took the helicopter there, and I called down to Medina, "This is Charlie One. I'm back and I'm ready to come in—"

"Negative."

"I'm up in the helicopter—"

"Negative! Go to Uptight and sit down up there."

Medina just wasn't taking risks, and I flew to Uptight again. I asked them, "Who's been hit?"

"I'm not sure—"

"How many?"

"Eighteen—"

"But who?"

"I'm not sure—"

A terrible day. Six soldiers dead. And twelve soldiers crippled. And me: I was different too. I looked off of Uptight, and it wasn't beautiful now. The rice paddies weren't green now: I only saw, *They're high. A man could be lying there. And kill me.* A village wasn't a little village now: it was houses, and I saw smoke from the third on the right. I saw people and—*They're looking at us.* I saw fishing boats, and I thought, *Are they fishing there? Or bringing supplies in? Is the Navy keeping its eye out? I wonder*: I saw just jungle now. I looked at every tree: at every bush and I asked, *Is the enemy there? Or there? Or there?* I knew I could defeat them if I met the VC eyeball to eyeball—*if*. I looked at everything hard now, and I asked, *Is that what's killing us?*

And then, I had this emotion inside me. Others call it a thousand things: the shakes, the sweats, to me it was simply *fear*. If you're falling, or if some screeching car is almost upon you, or if you're being shot at, I say that isn't fear. Or isn't chronic fear, the fear that's there in Vietnam. I hadn't ever had it, war stories didn't tell it, war movies didn't show it: chronic fear. It is like love, I think, as you're always aware of it and every tree is a new thing because of it. The fear in Vietnam is one that stands still: a time there becomes a tunnel over you, a trip through a horror house. I didn't have a fast heartbeat now: I had something mild. A mild panic inside me. Quite mild: but if I didn't find the VC soon, it could grow in me. It could overcome me. I knew, *I've got to find those people or it will strangle me.* Fear.

I think almost everyone in Charlie had it. The next day, I went off Uptight and it seemed like a different company now. It was dead solemn now: it did no childish horsing around when it went through a Vietnamese village. In December, the GIs had been infatuated with the Vietnamese children. No more: now as they reached a Vietnamese village and children said, "Give me," "Give me," and threw their arms around the GIs, the GIs just kicked them off and busted through. As they're supposed to! Intelligence said: if there are a hundred kids in a village, where are the men? They're getting the hell out of it. Or getting ready to zap us while we're tied up talking to nice sweet kids. I thought, *It's sad*: Intelligence had a VC code saying this was a VC tactic now. Intelligence told us, "Bust through. Get through to the goddamn village." You know? Those kids had been following us right to where we would RON. And been telling the VC, "They're there."

I didn't say, "Well, I told you so." It had taken the GIs three months with the Vietnamese to learn about them, but I didn't say, "You're wising up." In fact, I was disheartened about it. Someone would kick a Vietnamese kid: I couldn't be happy about this. Or someone would hit a Vietnamese girl. Or someone would use a Bowie knife to try to cut some of her hair off. Or walk around like an Indian with a few locks of hair hanging off him: I would think, *Big goddamn deal*. It accomplishes what? It only insults the Vietnamese girl and it doesn't do a damn thing else. The first soldier to do it I told, "Let the girl go."

"Well, I just want some hair."

"What for?"

"Well, the other platoons have it."

"Let the girl go."

After those days in Vungtau, I saw how hostile the GIs were getting to Vietnamese. Right off, I had acute problems when the Vietnamese at a marketplace tried to sell us Coke, beer, cigarettes, soap, and some niceties such as silk pajamas for sending home. One young girl, a GI started to grab at. To drag as though telling us, "Haha, I got myself one. Is it okay to rape her too?" One of the little concession stands, a GI kicked over and started to stomp on. I heard a woman scream, and I told a sergeant with me, "Get him off Mamasan's stuff." I understood the GI, though. Hell, all of the mamasan's things were his: he had originally given them to a Vietnamese kid, or someone had. He was, of course, frustrated, too: if you're in Vietnam you've got to blow steam off. If you're a GI who has lost eighteen friends in a minefield with a Vietnamese village a few hundred meters away —well. You think, *Why didn't the Vietnamese signal us? Why didn't the Vietnamese tell us, "Hey, there's a minefield there." Why didn't the Vietnamese help us? Or Christ! Or simply say to us afterwards, "We're sorry about it."* Never: they sat in front of their hooches talking, twiddling thumbs, and all saying, "Gee, I see an American unit," "I wonder what it is doing," "*I* know what it is doing," "Hahaha." If these people won't lift a finger, a GI will say, *Goddamn them. I'm here to help these people, and they couldn't care less.* And so a bad feeling sets in.

We didn't punish the GIs for it. Someday, there would be VC with sticks and stones and frying pans and weapons: someday soon, and the GIs would need a high fighting spirit. A high morale, and if just cutting hair off a Vietnamese or beating hell out of a prostitute or just being *with* a prostitute or throwing away an empty water can, a bandolier, or a rifle: if just being human beings did it, I would forgive it. Or hell, I wouldn't have had a GI left.

As for me, I didn't touch a Vietnamese if I didn't have to interrogate him: I put in a little incentive, then. Say if I was at a village and I was fired on. But everyone there was a nice sweet person like on a Southern porch. All right, I would get a head honcho or—I don't know, I'd get someone there, and I would ask him, *"VC adai?"* Or *"VC adoe?"* It may be fictitious, but I was told these are Vietnamese sentences for "Where are the VC?" They are the only sentences I know, *"VC adai?"*

"No bitt," "I don't know."

"VC adoe?"

"No bitt," "I don't know."

I had a GI interpreter with me: Specialist Grzesik. In Ha-

waii, Grzesik had taken forty-five days of Vietnamese: of
Saigonese dialect, and up north he would always tell me, "I
can't understand him." But you don't need an interpreter
for "I don't know," and that's what the Vietnamese told us.
It frustrated us. That someone could shoot an AK-41 and
people wouldn't know it. The soldiers would tell me,
"Strange goddamn place! I could of swore that a VC was
shooting at me." I couldn't go to Medina again or to higher
and say, "I'm back."

"What did you ask the Vietnamese?"

"*VC adai.*"

"What did the Vietnamese tell you?"

"*No bitt.*"

"You're an Army officer, aren't you—"

I knew I would hear it. An officer ought to get results:
okay, so I sometimes shook up a Vietnamese who kept telling me, "*No bitt.*" I just popped him as I asked him, "*VC
adai?*" To begin with, to *touch* a Vietnamese head is de-
grading him. And everyone did it: Medina leapt at a Vietnamese once and he even wrestled with him. And scared
the living hell out of him, actually. *God*, the Vietnamese
may have thought. *It's the big dragon from the sea.* Another
time, Medina put a Bowie knife to a Vietnamese's finger,
"*VC adai?*" And his ear, "*VC adai?*" And then fired an M-16
twelve inches over the Vietnamese's head. Six inches over.
Three inches over—

"I member of Geneva convention," the Vietnamese said.
In English! "I demand—"

"Bullshit," Medina said.

"—you report name to International Red Cross. I demand—"

"*VC adai?*" Medina said. "You answer that. And *then*, I might report you." And just popped him one.

He was lucky he wasn't sent to Task Force. At military police, they had an Army field telephone with a crank on it. They would wire up a Vietnamese's wrists and (as they called it) would ring him up. They had a POW cannon if that didn't do: a fifty-five gallon drum for a Vietnamese to squat in the water in. Ninety volts, and it would shoot the POW out: it even could kill him. Soldiers knew lots of the physical ways to interrogate. I saw them tie a Vietnamese to a cross once: a little bamboo one. And dunk a Vietnamese in a well, another time. I heard of a Vietnamese once, he was dropped in a well after someone gave him a few live grenades. He could let go and blow himself up or let himself drown, that's all. And then the American said to another one, "See what I did to Joe there? *VC adai?*"

Now, if I had seen anything like it, I would talk! I'd answer before I was even asked. I once saw an intelligence man, a Vietnamese who just stepped off a helicopter and everyone there went limp. Because god! He was bad, and the Vietnamese knew it. He just spoke softly. He just touched a Vietnamese gently. And the Vietnamese started sobbing—gosh, but I was impressed. I told myself, *This man! He just stands here and people cry*. As for me, I didn't care to make people cry, but I was an Army officer and I had to get that intelligence. I would pop a Vietnamese in the mouth, sometimes. If it threw him, I stepped on his ankle bone and I started to grind it. I may have killed a Vietnamese once: a horrible thing, but I have to live with it. He was kneeling, and I was kicking him as I asked him the "*VC adai*" and the "*VC adoe*." I meant to break some ribs, but he turned black and blue and he just passed out. A medic said, "You busted his kidney." I never shot a Vietnamese, but I did make believe to. I would say, "*Cacadow*," or "Kill," and I'd take the Vietnamese out behind the house. I'd fire, I'd let a GI give a good-sized scream, and I'd ask another one, "*VC adai?*" It never worked: the VC knew— the Vietnamese knew I was joking about it. They still told me, "*No bitt*."

Nothing worked ever. Had it, I guess the newspaper stories might say, "Calley was a tremendous man. He broke the Vietnamese's legs, or ripped their nails out, or cut their fingers off. He learned where the VC camps were, and he saved a thousand lives." But it didn't work, so I was a dummy and I didn't continue it. One day, Grzesik, the GI interpreter, told me, "It's futile. I don't want to ask these questions." I kept beating the man but god! It hit me that night like a ton of bricks, I realized, *Grzesik's right*. I was torturing them, and I wasn't getting answers. I was just hurting them, and I stopped it: I stopped as fast as I'd started it. I went along, and I didn't even say, "*VC adai*," anymore. I realized, *I've been foolish*. I had been asking everyone where the VC were: I had been talking to VC myself! That is why everyone said, "I don't know." They weren't about to tell me, "I surrender."

At last it had dawned on me, *These people, they're all the VC.* I realize, there are Americans who say, "How do you really know it?" Well, I was there. I made decisions. I needed answers, and I didn't have a more logical one. We had an AO of five hundred square kilometers, and if those people weren't all VC then prove it to me. Show me that someone was for the American forces there. Show me that someone helped us and fought the VC. Show me that someone wanted us: one example only! I didn't see any. A story: I used to see wicker baskets everywhere. And every basket was upside down, I could see. Strange: but Intelligence said if Americans are around, it's a VC signal to turn their baskets upside down. And everyone's basket was upside down.

My superiors sure as hell weren't telling me, "These are nice people here." We had some wounded girls once, and Medina said, "If they weren't VC, they wouldn't be here getting shot at." Our task force commander—well, the Colonel's dead and I'd rather not say. His staff, though, said it's a VC area and everyone there was a VC or a VC sympathizer. "And that's because he just isn't young enough or old enough to do anything but sympathize." I even heard a brigadier general say, "My god! There isn't a Vietnamese in this goddamn area! They all are VC!" I believed it. And as soon as I understood it, I wasn't frustrated anymore. I wasn't fooled anymore. I went through the villages, and I didn't say, "*VC adai,*" anymore. I said, "How are the VC today?" And, "You're a VC, aren't you?" And, "Everyone here is a VC, isn't he?" The people would tell me, "No no. We love the GIs. We give you water—" Hell, if I let them they'd poison the water, too. I didn't listen: I just walked on.

I had no love for these people now. I did have a few weeks earlier, but it had been slowly driven out.

We made a new assault on Mylai One in March. Remember the first one? How we were fired on from behind by "civilians" in Mylai Six? So now we landed outside of Mylai Six and were fired on from behind by "civilians" in Mylai Five. The soldiers said, "God, they're behind us," after which it was simply hell.

All this happened to Bravo company, the assault force that day. Our company was to the north again, and we were still milling there when it was called off. At noon, I got a radio call and Medina said, "So much for the second punch," and I took everyone to Uptight again. We had blown it again, and I went to walking around again. To getting guys up at seven. To listening to Medina tell me, "Calley, swing out and check out the village there." To listening to GIs ask me, "What in the hell for?" To never stopping, to hitting the ground when a VC fired, to hitting mines, to losing guys to dysentery, hepatitis, malaria: it had become routine now. I had come to Vietnam with forty-four men: I had twenty-four now.

At night, we would have to dig in. I'd have a beer, perhaps, and I would call in the defcons: the defensive concentrations, and I'd try to remember the damn registration numbers, the 711833 zulus and so on. I hated those, and I hated having to go waking guys up and asking them, "Who is on guard here?" I'd go to sleep eventually, and god:

"Charlie One. This is Diamondhead Six," the Colonel.

"Diamondhead Six? This is Charlie One."

"Charlie One, I've got a situation here. I want you to get your troops up."

"What's up?"

"You're wasting time, Charlie One. I want you to get your troops moving out."

"At what time do—"

"*Don't be smart with me, Charlie One! Right now!*"

It had become routine: the Colonel sending me shackle codes of coordinates, me then decoding them by a flashlight and just thinking, *Well, if I'm shot I'll save a hell of a walk*, the sergeants all asking me, "What in the hell's going on," the troops all screaming at me, "Goddamn it! We walked all yesterday night, we walked all yesterday day, we got to walk tonight now? Don't they know, *We got to get some sleep?* Don't they have any respect for us—"

"Troop," I would say, "I don't give a damn if you go or go back to sleep: so shut up!"

Two o'clock in the pouring rain, and we would be moving out. Be starting another day by walking either in Indian style in that famous formation *hi diddle-diddle and file down the middle* and by being ambushed, or by keeping off trails and by falling into the holes, walking into the trees, falling into the paddies, stepping over the cliffs— We just were playing games here, and we were being laughed at. Cowboys, the Vietnamese called us. Boys with the pretty faces. Boy scouts.

Once, we came to a village where we really caught a VC, rifle and all. I don't exaggerate: I pulled him out of a secret room. He had gone through a crack, around a corner, and then behind a fireplace with an AK-41. We found him, though, and I sent him to military police with a manilla tag on: name, location, etcetera, and on the back something like "Found behind false wall." You won't believe it: I caught him again a few weeks later. In the same village again. And wearing the same manilla tag as though telling us, "I've been interrogated, and I'm okay. I've got a ticket to ride!" Of course, he had taken charcoal and he had crossed out the "Found behind false wall." I told myself, *God. He has probably killed two or three of us. And the MPs didn't do a damn thing with him.* I went there angry: I said, "My god! I didn't call him a VCS," a VC suspect. "I said a VC!"

"Well, fine. So why didn't you go and shoot him? I can't," the MP said. "I'm at headquarters with the Geneva people on me."

"But you've got a POW camp—"

"A prisoner, I've got to give him a bed, a blanket, a pillow, and three square meals every day. And so many cubic meters space: I haven't space."

"But god! The guy's a VC—"

"All of these guys are VC. But they could tell me, 'I'm Egyptian,' and I'd have to believe them. We killed a man yesterday: the POW cannon zapped him. We aren't allowed to use coercion now."

"But if he's got an AK-41—"

"I'd love to be in the field with you. I'd take every prisoner and I'd kill every damn one. Do it, Lieutenant, or you're going to see these people back."

I didn't tell the GIs that: but I didn't have to. From then on, they would tell me, "My god, sir. Why don't we do something to these people?"

"What do you want to do? Send them to Task Force? They're going to send them back out."

"My god, sir. I want to do *something*."

"Well, what do you want to do, troop? Talk to these people? Go in and pacify them?"

"Hell no! I want to go in and shoot them!"

I wouldn't let the GIs do it. I even hinted about the manilla tag guy, "He might be an Army intelligence agent." I just couldn't let the GIs kill without having orders to. Suppose an American politician told me, "That's horrible! If that woman was a VC, why didn't she have her uniform on? Her weapon?" I couldn't authorize that, and yet— I thought about it. I was troubled about it. My duty in our whole area was to find, to close with, and to destroy the VC. I had now found the VC. Everyone there was VC. The old men, the women, the children—the *babies* were all VC or would be VC in about three years. And inside of VC women, I guess there were a thousand little VC now. I thought, *Damn it, what do I do? Hack up all these damned people? Pull a machete out and kkk—? Chop up all of these people?* That's what the VC themselves will do. Kill the rear echelon people: ones in the quartermaster corps, the transportation corps, the ordnance corps—

Everyone said eliminate them. I never met someone who didn't say it. A captain told me, "Goddamn it. I sit with my starlight scope, and I see VC at this village every night. I could go home if I could eliminate it." A colonel: he told me about a general's briefing where the general said, "By god, if you're chasing dead VC and you're chasing them to that village, do it! I'll answer for it! I'll answer for it!" The general was in a rage saying, "Damn, and I'll lose my stars tomorrow if I tell those politicians who haven't been out of their bathtubs that." Americans would say, *It's wrong,* if American women fought in Vietnam, but the VC women will do it. And the VC kids: and everyone in our task force knew, *We have to drop the bomb sometime.*

And still people ask me, "What do you have against women?" Damn, I have nothing. I love them. I think they're the greatest things since camels. And children: I've nothing against them. "Why did you kill them?" Well damn it! Why did I go to Vietnam? I didn't buy a plane ticket for it. A man in Hawaii gave it to me. "Why did you go? Why didn't you go to jail instead?" Oh, you dumb ass: if I knew it would turn out this way, I would have.

The day we got orders to My-lai, we had services for Sergeant Cox. A well-liked soldier in Charlie company—well, we never lost a soldier who wasn't liked. I haven't the vaguest idea why he had picked up a 105 artillery shell with a bamboo handle on it. A lieutenant said, "*Put the goddamn thing down,*" but it went off: it blew him to hell. It had been booby-trapped.

We had services at our task force headquarters camp, a camp known as Dotti. We got ourselves halfway decent: shirts on and trousers bloused, to sit around an old artillery emplacement on 55-gallon gasoline drums full of dirt, sand, or cement, or on some sandbag bunkers: a bleachers, sort of. Medina kept yelling at us, "Calley! Where are your people?"

"Sir, they're all here."

"Brooks! Where are your people?"

"Sir—"

It soon dawned on Captain Medina, *The company's here.* We had been out in Vietnamese villages for three months now. We were together and god! We were fifty or sixty soldiers short.

A chaplain began the usual memorial service. I just despised it. The soldiers would tell me, "We would like one of the chaplains, sir. It's secure here—" But they wouldn't go: they would just go to Dotti and say, "Sergeant Cox. A really great guy! He's dead and I'll give him—" I forget it. "Spiritual aid." I thought, *And what if Cox wanted his spiritual aid yesterday?* A man's spiritual aid, it should be there whenever he needs it. I thought it was lousy the chaplain telling us, "He was a great soldier, and I will dedicate this to Sergeant Cox: *the Lord is my shepherd, I shall not want—*" I wasn't listening, really. The services had become stereotypes for me. A prayer and the Twenty-third psalm and a prayer and a Bible verse and a prayer and a silent prayer and a prayer and the chaplain would say, "He died in defense of America." It had become a drag, really: a morbid thing, we had enough low morale without thinking, *God, another one meeting his maker.*

We had been stirred up enough at Cox's death: I wasn't there, but I've read about it in Seymour Hersh. People in Cox's squad had gone around kicking sandbags, according to Hersh, and calling the Vietnamese dirty dogs. And wanting revenge.

Moments after, a GI shouted, "Something's moving," and the squad opened up with rifle fire. The suspect fell.

I believe it. GIs are human beings, and if they think, *I'm frustrated, I just can't take it,* they're going to lose their mind or get rid of it. Psychiatrists say to women every day,

"Go home. Go hit your husband's head with a rolling pin. Get rid of your damned frustration." And damn! A squad leader's dead. And a GI knows, *It's a Vietnamese booby trap.* And a Vietnamese moves and a GI says, *Okay, Sergeant Cox. We'll get him.* Or her: it was just a woman, apparently.

> The woman was still alive. Someone suggested calling in a helicopter. "She don't need no medevac," one GI exclaimed, and shot her. Someone else stole her ring.

I can believe that, too. A woman has a nice-looking ring on. She's dead: she doesn't need it anymore. And a GI thinks, *Hell, a VC would dig her teeth out.*

I doubt if Medina punished anyone for it. He had a hundred troops left: he had them working double time and getting half the sleep afterwards. And there's the trauma of death on them night and day. And if a squad suddenly blew its mind: if it kicked a Vietnamese kid or killed a damn innocent woman that he hadn't any compassion for—god! Medina was going to criticize them? Or court-martial them? Or put them to death? He had the Colonel telling him, "We may have replacements in April. Or May. Or June." And every sergeant telling him, "Captain Medina! I need some people! We got an attack tomorrow: I haven't the people to do it!" Hell, Medina wasn't about to lose those men. He had to keep a combat-effective unit.

"He died in defense of America," the chaplain said.

And after the prayers for Sergeant Cox, the Captain stood

up to say some niceties and say, "We still have a war to fight, everyone. We haven't time to cry about this. It's over with. It's done with. Forget it: especially since we are going to Pinkville tomorrow." Pinkville: that was our company's name for Mylai One. On maps it was colored pink, and as soon as Medina mentioned it the troops sat up. Or *woke* up. Medina went on, "We're going after the 48th battalion. And they outnumber us two to one. At *least,* and there will be heavy casualties tomorrow."

I thought, *Hell. He didn't have to say it. Everyone knew it*: Alpha and Bravo companies had been there before. And men had their heads blown off or their balls blown off: I mean literally, or were vegetables now at Walter Reed, in Washington. As soon as you're close to Pinkville you're in a wall-to-wall minefield. And you're being fired on from front and behind: from the "civilians" in Mylai Six. The old men, women, and children there are in that battalion, really: the irregulars. And they're firing, and they're arming mines, and they're triggering them. And if they're with you as POWs, they're pulling pins out of your damn grenades. And you're saying, "God! They're everywhere," and you're running in every whichway. And you're dying like flies: it happened to Alpha, it happened to Bravo, it would happen to Charlie tomorrow.

To me. I knew now, *It's a lottery here. It's a man taking names from a ballot box.* A good guy, or bad guy, or just anyone could get it. By being just at the wrong place at the wrong time: that's all. And what could be wronger than to be in Vietnam in March, 1968: in Tet? It was stupid, it was idiotic to use a company against a battalion tomorrow. It was against the Manual. Of course, if I'm told, "Go to China tomorrow alone. And annihilate it," I have to go. With gusto! Or go to Pinkville without asking, "Why?" A second lieutenant is not anyone to ask it. Go let the General ask it, I could just go to Pinkville and try. And pray: I knew it's a big deal dying. It happens once in a lifetime, but I really wanted to put it off.

I really might. We had a Plan, Medina was telling everyone now. And went to a Jeep: and taking a shovel out, he drew in the sand beneath him a map of our operation area. From left to right, this was Mylai Four, Mylai Five, Mylai Six, and Mylai One: or Pinkville, on the China sea. Pinkville now was the VC basecamp, Medina said, but we didn't want to get fired on from behind and we would start at Mylai Four. And continue to Mylai Five, Mylai Six, and Mylai One. "We mustn't let anyone get behind us," Medina said, as I remember it. "Alpha and Bravo got messed up because they let the VC get behind them. And took heavy casualties and lost their momentum, and it was their downfall. Our job," Medina said, "is to go in rapidly and to neutralize everything. To kill everything."

"Captain Medina? Do you mean women and children, too?"

"I mean everything."

Now, I know Medina denies this, and I know why. He's married. He has children, and their benefits end if Medina is sentenced for it. He came to my trial at Fort Benning, Georgia, in March, to testify that it had happened this way, "Captain Medina? Do you mean women and children?" "No. You have to use common sense." But there were a hundred witnesses, and no other witness heard him say, "You have to use common sense." One eyewitness was Sergeant Schiel: "A person, I don't know who, a person sitting below me brought forth the question, 'Do you mean everything?' Medina said, 'Everything. Men, women, children, cats, dogs: everything.'" A soldier whose name was Moss said, "He said, 'It was *all* VC and VC sympathizers,'" and Flynn said, "He replied, 'Kill everything that moves.'" A total of twenty-one soldiers testified for me. "He told us that everything, we was to kill it," Sergeant Cowen. "He didn't want to see anything living but GIs," Kinch. "We would leave nothing walking, crawling, or growing," West. "He said everybody should be destroyed," Meadlo. "Anybody was to be killed," McBreen. "We were to kill all VC," Sergeant Bacon.

"Could this be a woman?"

"Yes. It could be a woman."

"Could this be a child?"

"Yes. It could be a child," Bacon said. "*Anything*, whether it be men, women, or children," Fagan. "There were no innocent civilians in Mylai. Men, women, children," Haywood. "We were told to destroy it," Sergeant Maroney.

"Did this include the inhabitants?"

"Yes sir," Lieutenant Aloux.

"Men, women, and children?"

"Yes," PFC Glimpse. "To destroy: that was it," Oliver. "Along with its inhabitants," Bernhardt. "To kill all inhabitants," Martin. "We were supposed to destroy: that is, kill everything," Lloyd. "Kill everything," Partsch. "Kill anything," Lamartina. "Kill everything," Gonzalez—"Men, women, and children."

In Georgia, the Judge called this an illegal order. So be it: except that at Dotti there were a hundred troops, and I don't think anyone said, "I arrest you, Captain Medina." Or even, "I won't obey it, Captain Medina." In Georgia, the GIs testified that an order's an order: obey it. One witness said, "No matter how asinine it may be." Another, "If an officer tell you to stand in a highway on top of your head, you've got to obey it." I know at OCS, we were simply told, "You love pizza, don't you, Candidate Calley. Take it—" "Throw it—" "Rub it—" But do it! And don't ask why. An illegal order: I never heard about that at OCS. Is a pizza pie in a US government bedsheet illegal? It's illogical: it defaces a US government bedsheet. Is an atomic bomb on Hiroshima illegal? It kills children too.

I know you'll say, "All right: if Medina said to kill everyone in Atlanta, would you?" And someday an Army officer *may*, the way this country is going now. I say this: if this were a hundred years ago, if I were a Union lieutenant and if Sherman told me, "Kill everyone in Atlanta," I guarantee I would have to. I once got a letter on Mylai saying, "My god! Why are the *Yankees* upset?" It said in the Civil War, the Yankees were up against guerillas too. All the South's men, women, and children were out to defeat them. A very smart man in Missouri said, "If the Yankees come through here, do whatever you can. And poison the horses, and poison everyone's food. And invite the GIs—" I mean, "And invite the Yankees in, let them sleep with all of your daughters, and if they're in the latrine for a pee: then shoot them. Let them believe you and kill them." The same as Vietnam: the people became guerillas then. And used unconventional warfare: but the North wasn't about to sit in its trenches worrying, *Gee, can I feed my horses here?* It wasn't about to live afraid, and Sherman said if they wouldn't let the Army be, then there wouldn't be a Southerner left. He ordered his men to burn, to kill, and as soldiers say: to rape, pillage, and plunder the South. And there was no stopping him. The tactic worked.

If you're a Yankee, you'll tell me, "Sherman's great," and you'll put a statue of Sherman in Central Park. As for me, I'd hate to see a monument to Calley's March to the Sea. But damn it! Sherman knew the solution to unconventional warfare. And used it: and there's unconventional warfare in Vietnam, too. A committee of Congress said, "The 'civilians' in Mylai were there to aid the enemy or his cause." As long as they weren't too young: I agree. But when is a Vietnamese too young to pick up a straw? Four? Three? Two? If the straw is a "safety" in a VC mine—if a Vietnamese pulls it and we're anywhere near it, I say that's aiding the VC cause. Our task force intelligence man, Captain Koutouc—*K'toosh*—had a VC list, and some little children were on it: I learned about that in *Playboy*. An article by another intelligence officer:

> The list contained names of two-thirds of the population. It listed the VC guerillas to chairmen of VC farm organizations. The list did not overlook the VC girls and the VC boy scouts.

It had come from the Central Intelligence Agency.

> CIA coordinated Operation Phoenix—the systematic elimination of VC supporters. To the CIA, execution was an acceptable means of systematic elimination.
>
> Koutouc was given the blacklist for Mylai. He had it with him on March 16. After the massacre, the CIA received praise for Operation Phoenix, for they had eliminated the VC infrastructure.

Medina was never praised for it.

Medina told us, "Kill everything." It made sense: it made as much sense as any of Charlie company's missions the last quarter year, and I didn't question it. We could just get to Pinkville no other way. We *could* use CS tear gas if gas weren't against the Geneva rules. Or guard everyone if Medina had a few thousand troops. Or let them escape: the

Vietnamese and the VC battalion too. I was the senior platoon leader, though, and I say: if I had been captain then, I would have said, "Kill everything," too. In fact, I spoke to Medina earlier that day. We had coffee in Dixie cups and Medina said, "We are going to Pinkville tomorrow."

"For keeps?"

"We are starting back at Mylai Four."

"All right: I'm not going to play around," I said. "I'm not going to let anyone get behind us."

"It's your show."

I worry sometimes now. I lie awake, and I think of Mylai and say, *My god. Whatever inspired me to do it?* But truthfully: there was no other way. America's motto there was "Win in Vietnam," and in Mylai there was no other way to do it. No wonder an Army officer is so aggravated today. He has trained hard to forget, *To kill a man's wrong.* He psychs himself up, and someone tells him, "Okay! Get your people up! Get ready!" And getting ready, he has some headaches such as a GI saying, "I had a baby, sir," he gets ready, though, and the Man says, "Stop! You aren't ready." *Damn, I haven't tried yet.* So the second time: so the same routine. "Stop! We aren't doing it." *Frustration,* and the final time he gets ready, he has that mission and he accomplishes it. "No no no! We didn't want you to kill anyone! We wanted to win their hearts and minds!"

My god. You shouldn't teach us killing then.

The briefing broke up. The troops went to supper: I didn't, I had too much to do. I got another map, I cut out the Mylai part, and I memorized it: the coordinates of the centers of Mylai Four, Five, Six, and One. I got the coordinates for Alpha and Bravo companies and the radio frequencies that day. I went to Medina's hooch for an order-of-battle briefing and to the military police: where the VC prisoners were. I said, "Any intell on Mylai?"

"Not much. If you want to talk to the prisoners—"

"All right."

I went to the tiger cage: a cage of ASP runway stuff that was sandbagged over. A dungeon: the POWs had to squat there. And get stiff, and if they escaped from it they could be caught: a tiger cage.

I squatted too, and I asked a VC prisoner, "*VC Quangngai?*" It meant—oh, I didn't know. A million things, "Are you a VC from Quangngai?" "Are there any VC in Quangngai?" "Are the VC about to hit at Quangngai?" It meant, I guess, "Are you going to answer me?" If so, I would get an interpreter and I would ask—I still didn't know. I would ask for the moon, perhaps. For his telling me, "The battalion isn't in Mylai One. It's in Mylai Four." Or Five. Or Six, and I would call the Phantoms in. A battalion there in a five hundred meter by three hundred meter area, the Phantoms could easily burn it. With napalm: I say anything but to send soldiers in and lose lives. And so I asked that man, "*VC Quangngai?*"

"*No bitt.*"

"VC number one?"

"VC number ten."

I shrugged. There was a POW cannon there: I might get us some intelligence that way. It had just killed a POW, though, and now the MPs were petrified: *It's illegal.* What if some autopsy shows that he was electrocuted? And someone investigates? "Well, we were interrogating him. And shining lights in his eyes. And using him as a filament—" No, they didn't want to go to Leavenworth for that damned war. And the POW cannon was half destroyed then. I knew, *No intell.*

I still hadn't eaten. I went where the MPs lived, and I saw a bottle of A-1 sauce. I asked them, "How did you get it?"

"PX."

"Mind if I use it?"

"No. Ah, Lieutenant? About POWs," the MP went on. "Our tiger cage is filled up. Brigade and Division are filled too. And the Vietnamese tell us, '*We* didn't capture them.'"

"So—?"

"So don't send us POWs tomorrow."

I didn't answer: hell, the MPs had always said it. I took the A-1 sauce, and I made pizza pies out of C-ration bread, C-ration cheese, and C-ration beef. I thought, *Anyone with an AK rifle, I will still send to Dotti tomorrow. For intelli-*

gence: a Vietnamese would really be safer tomorrow with an AK-41. I gave the MPs some pizza pies, we had beer and we turned on the armed forces television channel: I think the Miss America. No, that wouldn't be in March then. The Academy Awards? Or the Grammies: I didn't really watch, and I left telling the MPs, "See you." I should have but I didn't say, "I hope."

I went along the platoon perimeter. I knew, *We must be ready tomorrow. We must be sharp or—* Well, if we're ready we needn't worry. I asked the men, "Is everything ready?"

"Yes sir."

I woke up Sergeant Mitchell and Sergeant Bacon, "The men. Are their weapons clean?"

"Yes sir."

I woke up Platoon Sergeant Cowen: I had a thousand questions for him. "How are the C's? How are the RTO's batteries? The helicopters: who's on the first one? The second one? The—"

"Everything's ready, sir. You give the Top the promotion list?"

"The promotion list? I will tomorrow."

"And tell him I want a cot here, please."

"I will, Sergeant Cowen."

"And also. I got to get to Division soon, I got this shoulder—"

He talked of everything else but Mylai. I went to the second platoon leader's hooch: to Lieutenant Brooks's. And they had a poker game on! His playing cards and his MPC, or his military payment certificates, were on the ammunition boxes, and his RTO was asleep with a radio on him playing the Cream, perhaps. A card player told me, "Come in. Got any money?"

"No—"

"Three sixes. Get you a Bud?"

"No—" I told him. "I think I'll rack out."

I went outside again. It was dead silent there. It was dark out, and I got snagged on the concertina wire as I went through it. I knew, *I'm as ready as anyone can be*: I felt empty anyhow. I wanted to keep asking questions so I wouldn't think, *I feel empty*. Or maybe to get some honest answers. "Are you ready, troop?"

"No sir."

"I am not ready either. I will never be."

I admit it: I was afraid. I can see now, *Everyone was.* And everyone hid it: Calley, Cowen, Brooks. And everyone hid it a different way. I kept walking, but I looked up and said softly, "Help us to be good soldiers tomorrow. Help us to make the right decisions: amen."

And slept. The next day, I got up roughly at six o'clock. I put some water in a steel pot: a helmet, and I shaved with it. And washed my armpits and groin area to keep fungus off. I dressed, and I had chow: scrambled eggs, a creamed hamburger, coffee, and I drew water for six canteens. I put those and the C-rations into a rucksack, and I saddled up: a cartridge belt, the rucksack, a flak jacket perhaps (I can't really remember that), and a brassiere sort of bandolier of ammunition clips. A rifle, and I just really swabbed it: I had done everything there was to do. It's weird, I even combed my hair thinking, *Why in the hell am I doing this?* And put on a helmet over it.

The troops. For once, I didn't try to speed them up. Or chew their ass: I just didn't want the platoon pissed off. Medina yelled, "Get your goddamn people down to that helicopter pad!"

"I don't think they'll start the firefight without us."

"Get your people down, or I'll get someone who can!"

On the choppers: there the adrenalin started. We felt as automobile racers do: *A split second, and I might hit the very edge of disaster. Or pass it.* We had about twenty thousand rounds for our M-16s with us: four hundred every man. And fifteen thousand for our machine guns, and four hundred grenades for our M-79 launchers, and a dozen shells for our 81-millimeter mortar. The choppers around us had fire behind them: the M-5 grenade launchers, the rocket launchers, and the miniguns were on Mylai already. A minigun: a super machine gun, in a minute it can have holes in every square foot of a football field. It was just devastating fire! We saw the artillery hit: a battery four of 105-millimeter cannons at Uptight and a heavy battery of 155-millimeters and 175-millimeters at Dotti. We saw them hit on the treetops of Mylai. And the Navy had swift-boats for us with thirty-caliber and fifty-caliber machine guns. And mortars. If need be destroyers and, I think, the New Jersey, and the

Air Force its Phantom jets. And that, I think, was really piss-poor: the Phantoms if *need* be. I wanted the Phantoms ready to go! On the runway itself! I had said to Captain Medina, "I don't care if I get them after I'm dead!"

For remember. I didn't know if a VC squad, or platoon, or company—*what* was in Mylai Four. Or the goddamn battalion even. I only knew, *It is shooting at us*: I got that from the chopper pilot. He brought her in and shouted at me, "A hot one!" It meant, "We are under fire!" It meant a lot more, though, "I hope you'll make it. I hope *I'll* make it. I am not staying here! Get out!" I thought, *Well, here we go*, I got up, I jumped—I didn't move. I tried, I just forced myself, I jumped a few meters into the paddies under me. The troops jumped out of the chopper behind me. Ahead of us: Mylai Four.

I'm going to die sometime: I had always known it. Ignored it: and knocked on the door of death today, and I couldn't ignore it. The fear now: I was saturated with it. I *felt* it, I kept running but it took extra effort to. A bullet: a pretty good way to go, I knew. No fuss. No muss, I wouldn't even know it was hitting me. A mine: that's worse, to wake up and think, *Now, what did I lose? My legs: I still have my arms, though*, I would try to think positively. Of the great guys who run around, jump out of planes, hop up a mountainside with an artificial leg. I would think, *I'm out, I don't have to worry anymore*. I had that mechanism: and I kept running to Mylai Four. It whirled, it was like seeing a bomb burst or a person blow up.

The fear: nearly everyone had it. And everyone had to destroy it: Mylai, the source of it. And everyone moved into Mylai firing automatic. And went rapidly, and the GIs shot people rapidly. Or grenaded them. Or just bayoneted them: to stab, to throw someone aside, to go on. Supposedly, the GIs said, "Chalk one up," "Hey, I got another one," "Did you see the fucker die?" I didn't hear it: I just heard Medina telling me, "Keep going," and I said, *"Keep going! Keep going! Keep—"*

"**G**od," people say. "But these were old men, and women, and children." I tell you: I didn't see it. I had this mission, and I was intent upon it: I only saw, *They're enemy.* Of course, I still was in South Vietnam. I knew, *There are old men, women, and children in South Vietnam.* It was common sense: sure, but in combat there is damn little common sense.

To start with, we had come in the wrong way: I had been where the second platoon was to be. We had switched sides, and I had been called by Captain Medina, "Any body count?" I had seen bodies out in a tapioca patch: the artillery's doing. Or the grenades, rockets, or miniguns. Or ourselves: I didn't know, but I had said to Medina, "Six to nine bodies." He said to Task Force, "Sixty-nine bodies." In Mylai, the GIs had slowed up for hedges, bushes, trees, for fences, for houses: and then fired at GIs ahead, and I had thought, *God, we are just going to kill each other*. It's true: I hadn't heard any VC rifle fire. Or mortar fire, but I didn't say, *Gee, I can breathe easy now*. A cross-country runner doesn't say, *Gee whiz, I'm out ahead. I can slow up*— He keeps saying, *Keep going*.

Medina says now, "You have to use common sense." Well, I wasn't taught at OCS to use common sense: I was taught, "Do this! Do this like this!" In combat, if Medina had really told me, "Use common sense," I'd have said, "Sure, I'm going back to Hawaii." In December! To use saturation fire: to use rifles, rockets, cannons, mortars, miniguns, and machine guns on a little guerilla—hell, to go to Vietnam to fight him, is that common sense? It is America's strategy, though. To keep putting the "stuff" out: to kill everyone in Mylai before someone gets an AK rifle out. And still people tell me, "But these are old men, and women, and children." Now, *they* ought to have common sense. And give us a bullet which won't hurt the old men and women and children.

And babies. On babies everyone's really hung up. "But babies! The little innocent babies!" Of course, we've been in Vietnam for ten years now. If we're in Vietnam another ten, if your son is killed by those babies you'll cry at me, "Why didn't you kill those babies that day?" In fact, I didn't say, "Kill babies," but I simply knew, *It will happen*. I knew if I was in Mylai with twenty thousand rounds, if I didn't shoot at paper targets there would be men, women, children, and babies hurt. It's chaos in combat, and I couldn't tell the GIs that day, "Be careful now." We weren't there to coddle them now. Or be cowboys, or be laughed at. Or listen to people say, *"No bitt."* Not any of us! And we didn't deny it at Fort Benning, Georgia. A squad sergeant from the second platoon testified, "We complied with the orders, sir."

"Did you kill men, women, and children in Mylai Four on March 16, 1968?"

"Yes." A squad sergeant from the third platoon said, "We could see people running from the first and second platoon. We stopped the peoples, and one of the GIs asked, 'What are we to do with them?' I said, 'Well, everything *is* to be killed—' And one of the individuals opened up on these individuals."

"Did your entire squad fire?"

"I can't really say."

"Did you fire?"

"Yes. I figured, *They're already wounded, I might as well go and kill them. This is our mission.*"

"Well now. Men, women, and children?"

"Men, women, and children."

"And your estimate of the number?"

"Ten."

All the platoons did it. And the Vietnamese knew, *I'm obstructing them. I had better fight or get out of their way.* And fled: and the pilots outside of Mylai just devastated them. I've heard of as many as five hundred killed that day. It's possible.

As for me, a leader who is shooting them is doing someone else's job. Not his own: and I had just taken seven clips or 125 rounds with me. Mostly tracers, so I could fire one and say, "Follow my tracer." I had just had to fire twice in Mylai Four. I had been alone at a big brick house, and I had looked inside. In the fireplace there was a Vietnamese man. At the window another one—and I shot them, I killed them. And strange: it just didn't bother me. I had once had a BB gun, and I shot a sparrow with it. I cried then, but now? I thought, *Sonofabitch's dead, and I got a body count now*. The worst thing about it had been the noise. My rifle made noise. It went bang: and that was the worst thing about it. I can't answer those who say, "Man, how can you kill someone?"

"I don't know," I say. "Use a rifle, I guess. Or stab him. Or burn him. Or some other way. And you?"

"I couldn't kill anyone."

"Even if they would kill *you*?"

"I couldn't kill anyone."

"Well, you'll be a poor soldier then."

"I couldn't live with it."

A silly statement, I think. Most of America's males were in Korea or World War II or I. They killed, and they aren't all going batshit. They simply escaped it. The human mind: I think it has more defense mechanisms than it has smarts. As for me, killing those men in Mylai didn't haunt me. I didn't—I couldn't kill for the pleasure of it. We weren't in Mylai to kill human beings, really. We were there to kill *ideology* that is carried by—I don't know. Pawns. Blobs.

Pieces of flesh, and I wasn't in Mylai to destroy intelligent men. I was there to destroy an intangible idea.

To destroy communism. Now, I hate to say it, but most people know a lot more about communism than I do. In school, I never thought about it. I just dismissed it: I looked at communism as a Southerner looks at a Negro, supposedly, *It's evil. It's bad.* I went to school in the 1950's, remember, and it was drilled into us from grammar school on, *Ain't is bad, aren't is good, communism's bad, democracy's good. One and one's two,* etcetera: until when we were at Edison high, we just didn't think about it. Well: Mary did. Mary was a timid girl at Edison who still would evaluate things. Who if someone said, "Sex isn't good," she would try it and answer, "No, it's great," and if someone said, "Communism's bad," she would ask, "Why?" A friend of mine called her a communist once, but Mary simply told him, "I'm not," and sent him a Christmas subscription to— What is it? *Pravda?*

I wasn't like her. I was a run-of-the-mill average guy: I still am. I always said, *The people in Washington are smarter than me.* If intelligent people told me, "Communism's bad. It's going to engulf us. To take us in," I believed them. I had to. I was sure it could happen: the Russians could come in a parachute drop. Or a HALO drop or some submarines or space capsules even. It could happen today in Los Angeles, I guess, or in San Francisco. A surprise attack: the Russians on a direct trajectory to City Hall. To the head honcho and say, "Surrender. Or watch us kill every man, woman, and child here." And if the mayor hesitates for a moment, they do it! They line up a thousand people and kill every single one. And get the mayor on his knees thinking, *God. These people are horrible. These people are monsters. God, to kill little children!* The mayor would say, "I surrender."

They did it in Vietnam, the communists. I had once known the Vietnamese village chief at Dotti. A hard rugged man: a John Wayne, but I had seen how the communists beat him. He had come to me sobbing, screaming, carrying with him a large earthen water jar. In it I saw what looked like a lot of stewed tomatoes. Blood. And a jagged bone. And hair. And some floating lumps of flesh. The interpreter said, "It was on his doorstep today."

"What is it?"

"His son."

"Who did it?"

"VC."

They had won. They had done him in. Those people are monsters, and they have no qualms, no hang-ups, no holding-backs to the extremes they'll go to. I mean butcherings: this is what communism does, and we were there in Mylai to destroy it. Personally, I didn't kill any Vietnamese that day: I mean personally. I represented the United States of America. My country.

I came out of Mylai on the other side: the eastern side, and I saw some people ahead of me. Vietnamese, and Americans watching them: I understood why. One squad at Mylai wasn't supposed to kill everyone there. We had those mines to go through, and the Vietnamese people would know the way. Would know if a zigzag wire, a bamboo stick that is slanted west, or is slanted east—if any of these meant mines, and Medina had told me, "Save some of the people." I'd said to Sergeant Mitchell, "Save some," and clearly those were the Vietnamese ahead of me. In fact, I'm not even sure if I saw them: I knew I had ordered it, *They're there*. It was just incidental to me. I was indifferent about it, I *wasn't* indifferent about the VC bunkers there on the eastern side. We could be fired at from those bunkers, and I said to Sergeant Bacon, "Check them out."

Bacon said, "Roger." And went to the northern bunkers.

"Sir—" Sergeant Mitchell. "Do you want the others checked out?"

"Roger," and Mitchell went to the southern ones.

A call came from Captain Medina. "Where are you?"

"I'm on the eastern edge, and I'm checking the bunkers out."

"Well, damn it! I didn't tell you to check them out. Get your men in position."

"I have a lot of Vietnamese here," I said, or "I have a lot of VC—"

"Get rid of 'em. Get your men in position now." Medina knew, *We still have a VC battalion ahead. Any damn minute—*

"Roger," I said, and I started to where those people were. In the paddy ahead of me. At this irrigation ditch: a ditch that the Vietnamese get the water from. And were squatting there with a GI guarding them: PFC Meadlo. He was very afraid, I know. He thought, *Any minute, they'll have a counterattack. And pull on a piece of string somewhere. Or a chain somewhere or—* I know because he would testify so. I went up to Meadlo and asked him, "Do you know what you're to do with those people?" A damn illogical question. How in the hell could a PFC know what to do? *I* didn't know what to do. I may have thought, *Well, if Meadlo knows what to do, I won't have to worry about it.* A damn illogical question in this illogical place: in Vietnam. "Do you know what to do with those people?"

"Yes—"

And right then, I saw a GI with one of those individuals: a Vietnamese girl. He had hold of her hair to keep holding her to her knees. He had a hand grenade (I was later told) to threaten her little baby with. He wanted a blow job.

I ran right over. "Get on your goddamn pants," I said. "Get over where you're supposed to be!"

I don't know why I was so damn saintly about it. Rape: in Vietnam it's a very common thing. And Mylai, I've even heard that's a twelve-year-old in the photograph in *Life*. A soldier from the platoon that did it would testify about it. "There were girls in that group, weren't there?"

"I imagine there were."

"Didn't one of you molest one?"

"I couldn't say. He tore her blouse off, if that's what you call molest."

"One of you fired then, is that correct?"

"That's right."

"Why?"

"I figure, *He thought this was his orders. Kill everything.*"

"Was it his orders to tear the girl's blouse off?"

"I object—"

In the other platoon, a GI raped a girl, another was in her mouth, another was in her hand, soldiers say. And even say, "She waved goodbye." Well, I guess lots of girls would rather be raped than be killed anytime. So why was I being saintly about it?

Because: if a GI is getting a blow job, he isn't doing his job. He isn't destroying communism. Of course, if I had been ordered to Mylai to rape it, pillage, and plunder—well, I still don't know. I may be old-fashioned, but I can't really see it. Our mission in Mylai wasn't perverted, though. It was simply "Go and destroy it." Remember the Bible: the Amalekites? God said to Saul,

> Now go . . . and utterly destroy all that they have, and spare them not; but slay both man and woman, infant and suckling, ox and sheep, camel and ass.

But the people took of the spoil—

and God punished them. No difference now: if a GI is getting gain, he isn't doing what we are paying him for. He isn't combat-effective.

"Get on your goddamn pants," I said.

He didn't argue. He complied, and I went north to Sergeant Bacon. He may have had a few rapists too: I couldn't tell, he was still at those bunkers, anyhow. I told him to hurry up, and showed him a cemetery a hundred meters east.

"For your machine gun. And spread your men to the right of it."

"Roger."

And again. A call from Captain Medina, "What are you doing now?"

"I'm getting ready to go."

"Now damn it! I told you: Get your men in position *now*! Why did you disobey my damn order?"

"I have these bunkers here—"

"To hell with the bunkers!"

"And these people, and they aren't moving too swiftly."

"I don't want that crap! Now damn it, *waste* all those goddamn people! And get in the damn position!"

"Roger!"

I really moved. I said to Sergeant Bacon, "Get your people together right now! *Move out*," and I went south to Sergeant Mitchell. Telling the RTO, "Now shut the damn radio off," or anyhow thinking it. The screaming: I was sick of it,

Medina was right behind me and pulling my string. And the Colonel his?

I passed by PFC Meadlo. He still had the Vietnamese there. I didn't even stop, I said, "Damn it! You said, *I know what to do with these goddamn people. Get rid of 'em!*" I meant—hell, I didn't know, I didn't think this out. I meant, "Get rid of 'em." I meant, "Go wave a magic wand. And say, 'Disappear.' " I meant, "Waste them," but I didn't think of what *that* meant. If it meant to Meadlo, "Kill them," I must admit it: I had that meaning. I had those orders: "Get in the damn position." A hundred meters ahead, and the Vietnamese were all in the goddamn way. I wasn't playing games here! I said to Meadlo, "Get them on the other side of the ditch. Or get rid of 'em!"

"Roger." Or some affirmative word.

I didn't stop, I went on to Sergeant Mitchell. He had some stuff from the bunkers there, such as cartridge cases. And nothing much, and I told him, "Forget it! Do you see the three trees there? Set up your machine gun—" And then, I heard shooting near us: north of us. I said to Sergeant Mitchell, "And spread your men to the left: to Sergeant Bacon."

"Roger."

And went to where the shooting was. I went around a few bushes, and I saw people down in the irrigation ditch. And dead: and a few more still stepping in. I saw Meadlo there. And Dursi, "*I like kids, and I can't tell them, Go away.*" And the prosecutor says Conti. And Grzesik, "*It's fu-*

tile. I don't want to question them." And some others, and I fired into the ditch myself. A few rounds: I had those tracer rounds, and they're bad for the M-16. They're painted red: it peels off in the chamber, generally. You can jam, and I fired at the most a half-dozen rounds, at the most sixty seconds. At the whole mass, and at a Vietnamese just rolling away. Or crawling away, and I told the GIs, "Now damn it! Get over on the other side! In position!"

I was mad! To begin with, I had those mines ahead, and I had wanted the Vietnamese ahead of me. Not dead, and especially not in the goddamn ditch. What if I had gotten hit? And needed this to fight out of? I knew the GIs wouldn't *jump* in with corpses around, and I knew damn well *I* wouldn't. It's sort of a messy trench, and I was damn irritated about it. But mostly about the GIs themselves. I didn't want Medina bitching at me: I wanted them in position. *Now,* and I said to Dursi, "Hurry up. Get on the other side of the ditch before you're sick." He had an *Ohhh* look, as though he were hunting deer and he had looked in a dead deer's eyes. It had been dirty work: a GI's a human being, and I said to Dursi, "Move out." He testified later, "It was in a sympathetic tone." I suppose so.

Meadlo was someone else. A kick in the ass wouldn't humiliate him: it wouldn't even get him mad. And the GI just needed one. He was still shooting down at the dead people down in the ditch. On automatic (there is some madness in war, believe me). He was afraid, remember, and he may have thought, *If there's someone alive, he'll be after me.* He would testify later that he had kept switching clips and ("I imagine") crying. I can believe it: Meadlo was simply losing grip. I kicked him, I told him, "Get on the other side of the goddamn ditch."

"All right—"

"Now go!"

He stopped shooting. He got reoriented: a day later, though, he would become hysterical. He would step on a booby trap, it would take his right foot off, he would be just bananas. "My little girl. My little girl. Oh, what have they done? She's innocent—" As for me, I would get a powder burn and a rock in my throat: nothing much, but Meadlo would cry, "They'll get you, Lieutenant Calley. They'll get you, Lieutenant Calley. You've got to get out of Vietnam." I'd have a few tears myself: *I'm alive*, but mostly for Meadlo. A perfect soldier. He always obeyed me. He didn't say, "Why? Why? Why," as I didn't say to Medina, "Why?"

At the ditch again. It had a log across it: a bridge, and the GIs walked over it. Into position, and I went north to Sergeant Bacon. I told him to tell everyone, "No more shooting."

"We weren't shooting—"

"And this raping, too. The next time I catch—" I named the GI who wanted the blow job, "I will court-martial him and you too! So you better watch out."

"I wasn't—"

"Now get in position!"

"Yes sir, but I wasn't shooting."

I'm not really sure of the sequence now. I saw a man in a white shirt and shorts, and I questioned him, "*VC adai?*"

"*No bitt.*"

"*VC adoe?*"

"*No bitt.*"

I thought, *You people. I only want to communicate with you. Now what in the hell must I do?* I asked him, "*VC adai!*"

"*No bitt.*"

"*VC adoe!*"

"*No bitt.*"

You sonofabitch. And bam: I butted him in his mouth with my M-16. Straight on: sideways could break the M-16. He had frustrated me! He bled, but I didn't kill him: I wanted him to interrogate later. He was about the same age I was, twenty-four.

He was drop-kicked into the ditch by—I don't know who. On the other side, a "Skeeter" or a small helicopter landed, the helicopter pilot left and a sergeant told me, "He wants whoever's in charge." I went where the helicopter was.

Where the pilot was. He told me, "There's lots of wounded here." He didn't say, "Vietnamese wounded," or "American wounded here." But either way, it would be the third platoon's job: I was supposed to keep going on. "There's wounded here."

"Yes."

"So what will you do about it?"

"Nothing. Relay it to higher."

"I already did. Can you call for a Dustoff?"

"Can *you*?"

"I already did. But they don't respond."

"If they don't respond to you, they won't respond to me." The pilot left, and I may have said to my RTO, "He doesn't like the way I'm running the show. But I'm the boss," and I called Medina. "He doesn't like the way things are being done."

"Roger. Where are you now?"

"I'm just about in position."

"Get in the goddamn position. And don't worry about the casualties."

"Roger," and I went south again to Sergeant Mitchell. To check out the— Suddenly, I saw a man crawling near me. I shot and I killed him, I had my RTO check him, and the RTO said, "He was just a small boy." He had been crawling away: or pulling pins out of VC mines, I wouldn't know. I went on to Sergeant Mitchell, I checked out the GI positions, and I went to Sergeant Bacon. And checked out the GI positions: I was in position now. I was secure now. I didn't have to go on: I could come up with sense now.

I could evacuate people. Ahead, I saw ten old men, women, and children, and the Skeeter again. And that pilot again: I went over.

He said, "The civilians. Are you going to evacuate them?"

"The only way I have to evacuate them is a hand grenade." It was true: the Army had just given us the grenades and the M-16, that was all. I said, "*You* have the helicopters here."

He looked sort of surprised. As though thinking, *Gee, I guess that I do*. He had three: his small helicopter or Skeeter had two big Scorpions with it. And the Skeeter would look for the VC, and the Scorpions would hit the VC with rockets, grenades, and minigun fire. All morning long, and now the Skeeter pilot had the Scorpions come in. And take the old men, the women, and children. I helped him to carry them on: and then never saw the Skeeter pilot until it was fifteen months later. At the Inspector General's Office, in Washington. He was wearing a sports shirt then: a red plaid one. He said, "The second one," and I stepped out of an Army lineup.

I asked them, "Who's that?"

"It's someone. He thinks he knows you."

"Fine."

Now in Mylai. It was lunchtime now: I sat with the mortar platoon leader and the forward observer for the artillery that day. I had some fruit, and I made small talk. "How is everything going?"

"Fine."

"Getting beer in?"

"Yeah. I guess I'll request it."

"We can get together tonight. Where did you get the two little girls?"

"Back there."

"Where?"

"In the hooches."

I opened a C-ration cracker can. I dipped them in C-ration cheese for the two Vietnamese with us. One was about four. And silent, the other was four, perhaps, and as cute as could be. A doll, a red little dress and all. I fed them the C-ration crackers, but I didn't play: I knew, *They're cute and all.* But they'd be alone in a little while. And starve. And stay there and rot, I knew. And the rats—well, it wouldn't be too nice being involved.

I felt the temperature now. I took my helmet off, and I used my rucksack to lie back on. To relax on: I knew I couldn't be fired on. For thirty years, the Japanese, the French, the Vietnamese, the GIs had never been in Mylai and not been fired on. I felt no jubilation, though: I was dead tired. To be in all that hysteria, the Captain's talk, the choppers in, the terror out in the paddies outside of Mylai, the hours inside it: everything, and to stop is to come right down. To crash: I was never on drugs, but I think that to "trip" and to "crash" is a similar thing to a morning at Mylai or anywhere else. To be at D-day or Iwo Jima, to do that shooting and TV shit, and to stop is a similar thing, I'm sure. All your adrenalin's gone, and you ask, *Now, what have I done? I've killed lots of German or Japanese or Vietnamese people. Big deal.* I felt I could really cry now. I lay in that paddy, I felt extremely tired, and I looked at the village ahead of me: Mylai Five. A few minutes more, and we would assault it. And destroy it. So this is what war is. Big fucking deal.

Medina said, "What is the body count?" We sat on a log together a few minutes later.

It always aggravated me, the body count. I would say to Medina, "Three," Medina would tell the Colonel, "Six." He would double it. But anything went in a body count: the buffalos, cows, the Vietnamese, and I always wondered, *Who gives a flying*—? All right: the American people did. The reporters did. And the Army would tell us, "Everyone else has a body count. Why haven't you?"

"What is the body count?"

I said to Medina, "I don't know."

"What is your estimate then?"

"I don't know. Go to the village yourself. Or go over there to the ditch. And count 'em."

"Anything off the top of your head—"

"Oh hell. Thirty. Forty."

"Lieutenant Brooks?" Medina had all the platoon leaders there, and asked every one. He then called the Colonel, and he reported fifty for the first platoon, fifty for Brooks's platoon, fifty for the third platoon, fifty for the mortar platoon, fifty for the helicopter units, and fifty for the artillery. And maybe some for the headquarters troops: it appeared as one hundred and twenty-eight in *The New York Times*. Front page.

I didn't argue with him. I couldn't care less, and I sat and I talked to Lieutenant Brooks. "It'll be a hot damn day."

"Yeah. A hot one."

"We ought to shoot an azimuth on Mylai Five."

"Yeah—"

I heard Medina say, "Wait out." He was still on the radio to higher: to the task force, and it had some question, apparently. "The bodies," Medina asked us. "What percent were civilians?"

Brooks said, "How do you tell?"

I said, "They're all VC. Or they're all civilians."

Medina said, "They want a percent."

"Everyone's dead," I said. "So what percent were civilians this morning?"

"I don't know."

"Or what percent were VC this morning?"

"I don't know."

I thought, *You dumb ass. You already told us, "Everyone is."* "So classify them as civilians now. As far as I care."

"Well—" Medina went on. "What percent did the artillery do?"

"*You* tell them. You told them twenty percent a minute ago." Or less, really: fifty out of three hundred bodies.

At last, Medina called in twenty percent civilians. I *think*, I just didn't listen. And gave us another briefing on Mylai

One: on Pinkville. It was deserted now. The battalion had already left it. We wouldn't attack it, Medina said. We would just do the usual: go through the villages here and ask, "*VC adai?*" "*VC adoe?*" He said, "I don't want any shooting."

"Roger," I said.

My rifle. I drew back the bolt, and I cleared it: I knew, *The operation's over*. And that day, we hardly saw anyone in Mylai Five and Mylai Six. An old man. An old woman. A very attractive girl in a Saigon gown: I thought, *She's out of place around here*. About twenty people, and we simply asked them, "*VC adai?*" We didn't shoot them: the Vietnamese police came and did. One man, the Vietnamese shot in the skull, and it flattened out: it looked like a Halloween mask now. "You better guard him," a GI kidded me. "He might crawl away."

"I don't think so," I said. "He has a terrible headache."

Death: we were getting used to it. Sometime that day, a GI shot the Vietnamese in white shorts, apparently: I heard from my RTO, "He isn't in any shape to interrogate now." The next day, we saw a Vietnamese woman down on the ground moaning, groaning, and carrying on: just dying, and I gave her a cinnamon roll. But someone shot her: a day later we saw another one, a Vietnamese nurse, and I thought, *She's dead*. But no: simply knocked out. By the man I had said to, "Put on your goddamn pants."

"Well," someone asked him. "Is she a good piece of ass?"

"Hell, no. She is too damn dirty to screw."

The next day, we went north again, and we were on operations all of March, April, May, and June. The months of Operation Golden Fleece, of Operation Norfolk Victory, of Operation Dragon Valley—

We had an AO of two thousand square kilometers now. It says in *The Military Half*, by Jonathan Schell, the Army destroyed seventy, eighty, ninety percent of the province there. I can't say, "It isn't so." I know we destroyed villages and villages there. At first, we were doing it badly: we got trapped in the fire, the smoke, and everything, and we got burned too. We hadn't burned any villages in Hawaii, and we hadn't got the "destroy" part of "search and destroy" down pat, I suppose. We saw about one thousand bodies in March, April, May, and June. I can think of the paddies full of dead bodies of pigs, water buffalos, soldiers, civilians, women, kids: it was common, civilian bodies. For every soldier killed there, I thought that a hundred civilians were. In the paddies, the bodies would be a ghostly white, or would be swollen and be a dark brown purple color. The ants would be entering at the nostrils and working into the eyes. And there would be vultures too, if the villagers hadn't buried them or GIs had dug them up. To get any weapons around them.

We dug up many fresh graves. I got so I didn't mind it: I knew I couldn't say, "I'd kill a VC but just wouldn't dig him up." I became callous there, and I looked at a corpse as exactly that: a carcass. *It's dead and it doesn't exist now*, I told myself. It's nothing to feel sorry for, or remorseful for.

It's nothing, and I shouldn't worry about it. I was once in a perimeter near the China sea. It was night then: the sea rolling in, the moon ricocheting off it. And god: from out of the sand there suddenly came an arm, then another one, a leg, then another one! It looked like a picket fence now. I figured the VC had buried their dead in that shallow sand: and as the water rolled in and rigor mortis set in, the arms convulsed and were coming up. I discovered, *I'm not even scared.*

To be around death took a while getting used to. It was hard on the crispy critters: replacements, who we began getting in Charlie now. A crispy would come and be given a casualty card so Quartermaster wouldn't say, "God. What is this body's name?" A crispy would get a casualty card and say, *Gee, I just got here. And already*—and I'd try setting him at ease. I said, "Where do you live?" "Do you have a wife?" "Do you have kids?" The basic things, and I tried smoking and joking with him. It must be human nature, though, if someone's new to try scaring him. I thought, *It's horrible*, but the GIs would tell him, "Boy! Have we got some stories for you!" Or wait until the defcons came in and holler, "Oh god! We're getting hit!" Or anything: I once saw a flare go off, and I said, "What's this?"

"Oh, dumb shit here. He blew it."

"What?"

"Oh, dumb shit here, the VC can cut off his balls now."

"*What?*"

"Oh, *you* know about it, Lieutenant," and I would learn

how the GIs had razzed him. Had tied a flare to the crispy critter's shoe: I hate to say it, because it could burn the living hell out of anyone. And to the other shoe, the GIs had tied a trip-wire and told him, "Sit with your legs like so. Or the VC will sneak up when you're asleep. And cut off your balls."

"Get the damn flare out," I said.

The first of the crispy critters came in April: the first three. All night the GIs teased them, "See the mountain there? We go up it tomorrow," "We'll be in continuous combat," "We'll be annihilated, maybe." And they really juiced it, till every crispy critter was half scared to death. Now, there really was a mountain that day. We had to climb it with ropes, sometimes, and a crispy told me, "My ankle hurts. I can't make it." I couldn't argue: I had a chopper get him. Another one of the crispies couldn't keep up. I told someone, "Go get that dingbat there," but no. The man needed water, and it was hours before the choppers would come and "elephant rubbers" or five-gallon cylinders would be crashing through: and busting apart. He had prostration, and I sent him out: I now had one crispy critter with me. They weren't used to Vietnam: the heat, the hills, or the bullshit stories.

Or death. On the mountaintop there was a VC operating room. In it an English bicycle had been lashed down, and if you pedaled it a wheel would spin, a generator would spin, a light would light up the operating table. We got there, we saw that table and it had gobs and gobs of blood on it. The blood at the table's edge was an inch thick: coagulated, but in the middle it was still warm and wet. Outside was a potato patch with the patients that the VC had just massacred. Had had to leave back and had massacred: killed, shot in their eyes or between their eyes or behind their ears. The bodies, the VC had placed in shallow graves, three inches under. As rigor mortis set in, the arms had come through and Delta company had torn little deltas out of its toilet paper and C-ration cardboard and it had hung these on the fingers. Or it had written DELTA there or DELTA MEANS DEATH, or the "funniest" one was SEE—YOU SHOULD OF JOINED DELTA.

The third of those crispy critters couldn't look at it. He sat down under a tree and he told me, "Lieutenant? I got to get an emergency leave. I got this wife—"

"I can't do a damned thing *now*."

"And she's pregnant, and my mother's sick, and my dog's lame—"

Etcetera. He wasn't used to dead bodies: but if I let dead bodies bother me, I'd go bananas there. "I can't do a thing about it," I said. "Up with those bodies, everyone," and I had fifty of them checked out. One was still groaning at us, "Uhhhhh." We burned the VC hospital and we left him. He just died there. Or walked off: I didn't know.

It didn't bother the older soldiers, death. On their helmets, they had an ace of spades playing card, and they called themselves the Death Dealers. To listen to, they wanted to kill every man, woman, and child in South Vietnam. GIs said to use napalm, or low-yield atomic bombs, or a chemical on the vegetation there. Or to line up along the China sea and say, "Prepare to shake hands with your ancestors. We are rolling through." To kill simply everyone: and to get some oriental in San Francisco and to bring him in as President of South Vietnam. I couldn't believe the GIs meant it. They said so much tribble—trivial dribble there, to hear themselves talk and to tell themselves, *Gee, I can still put a phrase together*. What else was a GI to talk about? "I went on this operation today—" "I know. I was with you." If there's nothing to talk about that's new, a GI became a quick philosopher and would say, "God, if I go and kill everyone here, I could leave." *It's logical*, I had to admit it. *He isn't serious, though*, I said.

The generals said, "We must deprive the VC of their population resource." I've even seen in *The Limits of Intervention*, the Assistant Secretary of Defense. He said, "Our policy seems to be: destroy the villages, defoliate the jungles, and cover all of Vietnam with asphalt." I suppose next, I'll learn that the President said, "I'd rather be dead than red. So they're better off if they're dead." As for me, I still was a second lieutenant. I had to obey orders and to hope those people in Washington were smarter than me. But sometimes —well, I told a platoon leader once, "I can see it. Ten years from now, I'll kiss my wife and I'll say, 'Goodbye, dear. I have to go to testify at the war-crime trials.'"

One night, the VC captured one of us. I heard the GI scream all night: really echo, and I was seven clicks away. It was as though the VC had amplifiers there—but no. They wouldn't need any if they're pulling skin off *me*. I know I'd give a good-sized scream if I'm ever skinned alive. And bathed in a salt solution. And given water to stay alive and to scream, as that soldier was. We listened and we just cringed! At dawn, we went to the high poles that he had been strung on. His skin had been ripped from his arms, legs, and abdomen: all but his face, and the VC had taken his penis off. Horrible: but it had been worse simply hearing him. And asking, *What in the hell's happening? What in the hell inhuman, crude, and—* God, I had thought. We had better be winning or this wasn't worth it. Death. And death. And more death.

And that's what the thing was. We weren't winning in South Vietnam. I did damned well if I said, *I may have saved a GI today: I killed someone here.* But anything else, I couldn't say it to save my soul. My day in Mylai had accomplished nothing: the 48th had gone right back in. We were men in a pond pushing away the water: destroying things, and as fast as we pushed it away it rushed in. One night, we got orders to go to Mylai again: to Mylai One. To get on those choppers at dawn again, and to assault two VC fifty-caliber machine guns on the barbed-wired beach. I was fearstruck about it. I saw us in front of the fifty-calibers dying, and I thought, *What will I do? Be Audie Murphy? Assault those guns? Or help those dying men?* I even prayed: I didn't say, "Don't let us go, God," but I meant it. I almost tasted it.

The next day, a sergeant woke me. "Medina wants you."

"What time is it?"

"Eight thirty."

"God—"

It had been called off. At dawn, the Colonel had just refused to go: had refused or whatever colonels do, and wouldn't commit us against the fifty-caliber guns. We were lucky: in May he took three other companies in and took heavy casualties. And the radio told us, "Diamondhead's dead," the Colonel's helicopter and another one collided. And the VC still were in Mylai One.

I was really ashamed of us. The troops would say, "Damn, Lieutenant! How can the Army stop communism here? Everyone's communist." Or would tell me, "I'm not going anywhere today."

"Get your ass moving, troop."

"I'm not going anywhere, I'm tired."

"Get on your feet there, troop."

"Lieutenant, I'll whip your ass. I'm not going anywhere."

It wasn't only the first platoon. In the second platoon, a GI was walking point once and wouldn't go on. An officer pulled out a 45 and ordered him, "Go on or I'll kill you," "Kill me." The third platoon had a GI say, "I'm not going up it." A mountain.

"Oh?"

"I'm going in to Battalion."

Or twenty kilometers back in VC country: impossible. The third platoon leader said, "Gee, I would like if—"

"Nope."

"I need everyone's help to—"

"Nope."

The third platoon leader got on the radio telephone. And said, "Charlie Six. This is Charlie Three. I've got a man refuses to go."

"Bullshit! Tell him to go or goddamn it! Knock the shit out of—"

"Charlie Six. I suggest that *you* knock the shit out."

"Can't you control your men, Charlie Three? Wait out," the Captain said, and he called the Colonel. "Triumph Six. This is Charlie Six. I've got a man refuses to go."

"A coward? Tell him to go or I'll court-martial his ass."

"Roger, wait out. Charlie Three? This is Charlie Six. Triumph says—"

"I know, I monitored it."

"Charlie Three! This is Triumph Six."

"Sir."

"Now what is the problem there?"

"I don't have a problem here, sir."

"I hear there's a man refuses to go."

"That's right, sir. It's your problem, sir. He's walking back to Battalion."

"What! He'll be killed," the Colonel said. He wasn't,

though: he met with a Vietnamese patrol, and he made it. We went up that mountain and *we* had the shit shot out of us: another ten casualties.

The damn operations! The captain himself of Echo company wouldn't go and would sit at Battalion saying, "I'm sick of these operations." But me: I was still like a boy scout, and I went by *The Boy Scout Handbook*. I told myself, *I can do it: I can destroy communism here.* And one day, I was hot, I was tired, I had been sniped at, I—a Vietnamese jumped from a bush ahead of us. He ran to a village, but by the time we got there he wasn't there: just an old mamasan and a thousand kids. I got a Vietnamese interpreter, and I told him, "Get her to say where the VC are." So he asked her, "*VC adai?*"

She said, "*No bitt.*"

I said, "Well, where are the papasans for the babysans?" The one thousand kids.

"All papasans dead."

"Don't give me that bullshit!" I took the closest kid and I said, "Where is this little boy's father?"

"Big big bomb come. *Boom.*"

"Wait a minute." I got about twenty kids and I said, "Where is this little boy's father?"

"*Boom boom.*"

"And this little boy's?"

"*Boom boom.*"

"And this little boy's?"

"*Boom boom.* All papasans dead."

"Where are their mamasans, then?"

"*Boom boom.*"

I knew, *She's lying.* Her son, her husband, and everyone else was a VC there, and I said, "I won't stand for it. Say where the mothers and fathers are, or I'll shoot you."

I wasn't really about to do it: I might if I was provoked, though. I had been issued an M-16 and been taught to shoot it. Remember at Kent State College? I wasn't there, but if a junior officer said, "*Fire,*" I couldn't challenge him. A rifle: that's what the Governor gave him. And the Army gave me.

"I'll shoot you."

"Well, war is hell."

"What?"

"Well, war is hell," the mamasan told me.

The interpreter laughed, and I just laughed too. It was great: an American there with a Vietnamese mamasan, and she had won. I thought, *It's beautiful*: but I was also bothered, I was demoralized. I had this mental picture: communism, and it was something mechanical. It crawled along: it crept along and it engulfed people, it enslaved people, it chewed people up. I told myself, *I'll recognize it. And with rifles, grenades, etcetera, I'll dismantle it.* I told myself, *I'm superior*: sure, but I was confronting communism now, and I was inadequate. It wasn't any machine, and it wasn't anything that a weapon could stop. It was just something there in the mamasan's mind: a philosophy. And if I knew Vietnamese, if I could tell her, "I'm here to help you," if I could talk to her twelve months, I might destroy it. But now, I could brandish an M-16 and just say, "I'll shoot you." And she could answer me, "Tough shit," I should take my M-16 and stick it right up. I knew now, *I just can't win*. A rifle: what can it do? Shoot the philosophy part out of Mamasan's brain? If it misses, the children would hate me. And never forgive me. And become communist too: I'd like to see people refute it.

Understand. I was still for the Army's being here: I just wasn't for the tactics here. We had come to Vietnam with a blunderbuss, counting kills. We said, "We killed three VC," and that sounded horrible. We said, "We killed three *hundred* VC," and that sounded good! But all but three of those three hundred kills were the Vietnamese we were there to help: civilians. We went through the rubble later, we dug up their living relatives, and we tried telling them, "We are good guys. We are doing this for you. In fifty years —" Hell. In fifty years they'll be dead themselves. Or be blown apart: I once saw a Vietnamese hospital room. In which there was a woman in labor, a guy covered by napalm burns, and a double amputee: that's on the *first* of the bloody beds, and a few children, too. And underneath it a woman in labor, another amputee: and I mean before he had gotten his leg cut off. And a man lying there with his guts in a plastic bag: I thought, *Horrible*. The moaning, groaning, talking a mile a minute, and the horrible odor in it—! Have you ever smelled a dog kennel? I went in and thought, *It shouldn't be. It's against the law. It's immoral. Now, who put these people together here?* Well, America did. Our weapons did. I did.

Jesus, I wanted to help there. To build a big beautiful hospital, to put everyone in a separate bed, to get firehoses and go wash the damned place down. I know lots of people say, "Oh well. I'd rather that it's the Vietnamese not us." The domino theory: that we shouldn't make war on America's soil but on someone else's. I say, "Well, rolly rolly, I don't agree." To make mayhem out of Vietnam takes a hell of an evil bastard to do, I believe. A man that didn't want the blood on his carpet is killing his wife on mine. And killing my own wife in the process—damn! I would kick him out. I would kill him, or I would be his enemy from then on. The same in Vietnam: we weren't stopping communism here. We just were stomping communism *into* Vietnam, and it kept sprouting again with a thousand branches.

The soldiers knew it. Believe me: the professional soldiers were as against this war as anyone was. Or more: their entire lives were the Army. And they enjoyed it. They took a tremendous pride in it. And they wanted it "Outstanding," and Vietnam was tarnishing it. America told the Army, "We have to stop communism there. Or it will conquer all of Vietnam, Cambodia, Thailand, Australia—" Listen. Remember the story of Dr. Frankenstein? How he would make a superman with the world's smartest brain and the world's strongest body? To do unbelievable things? If it had saved a child, or thought up how to kill locusts, or—I don't know the problems then, but it would be a great hero, but it just killed and killed.

Do not blame the Frankenstein monster, though. The people of the United States did create the United States Army.

We were on operations for ninety consecutive days. We were ragged from the malaria, hepatitis, dysentery: I'd say we had eighty percent dysentery now. The troops saw the IG about it, the division surgeon pulled us in, the company had a hot meal, showers, clothes, and that night—well, I don't think a VC did it. But someone threw a gas grenade into the Colonel's hooch, and he sent us right back out. To a VC area and to those terrible mines.

I was disgusted with us. I told myself, *God, the Army's screwed up, the Army's fucked up, the Army's a bunch of losers here.* Go and take fifty guys off Manhattan's streets, Philadelphia's streets, Washington's streets, and Miami's streets, and you've got an Army company: two hundred guys. American guys and they've nothing better to do. Average guys, and they'll hurt the Vietnamese's *philosophy*? Now you're putting me on! You better believe that the Army's medicine isn't good, the VC have better medicine than we do. I had always heard how the VC went for the

Vietnamese hearts and minds. Went to a Vietnamese village chief and were polite about it. Asked him, "Is there anything that we can do?"

"Just don't go stomping over the rice paddies, please: the Americans always do it. And Jesus."

"We'll stop it. We'll put a few mines in the rice paddies for you."

"Please do." And that village chief now is a communist, and I don't blame him. He needs a little tranquility there. And the US troops are like ignorant clods: we go to Vietnamese villages saying, "Get out!" And herd the Vietnamese out as though they're cattle, and we dig their ancestors up and throw their ashes away. And tear up Vietnamese rice paddies—damn! A balanced diet of rice is all that those people have. I often thought, *A steak dinner, and we could convince hell out of everyone here.* I thought, *We better punt, or think up some better play.* And in June, I learned about the S-5.

It happened by accident. I had moved out of Charlie company to Battalion: a normal thing, and I had reported in. I went into the adjutant's acting bold, and I said, "What you got for me, chief?"

"I'm not a warrant officer: I'm a first lieutenant."

"Roger, sweetheart. What you got for me to do?"

"I think the Colonel wants you at Delta. As the platoon leader of—"

"I had enough of it! Give me the tree-sitting job."

"A tree-sitting job? We haven't a job like that."

"Yes you do. You have the S-5 job, and I'd like it." Because every time I saw an S-5, he wouldn't be doing a damn thing. Be sitting under a tree. Or reading a book. Or almost absolutely nothing. I said, "You haven't too many trees here, but I'll sit in the officers club for the duration."

"Well, the Colonel wants an S-5. But he told me, 'I want a good one.'"

"A good one? I've only seen an S-5 under trees."

"Do you know what an S-5 entails?"

". . . No."

So the adjutant showed me.

(1) Harvest crops. . . .

(2) Construct housing. . . .

(3) Construct, repair, or improve roads. Construct, repair, or improve railways. Construct, repair, or improve waterways. . . .

(4) Teach sanitation. . . .

(5) Give education. . . .

That's from the Army manual, and that's what the damned war needed! To do little things that the Vietnamese appreciate. To talk, to communicate, to listen, to help: to win over their hearts and minds. I told myself, *To hell with the sitting under trees*, and I told the Colonel—I may incriminate myself but I told him, "I'm tired of killing them, sir. I want that job."

"You're really serious?"

"Yes sir, I'm serious."

"It's one of our hardest jobs. A week with the Vietnamese, and I can't get an S-5 out of the officers club or his head back out of a bottle." But the Colonel told me, "I need one."

"You got yourself an S-5."

"You mean *sir*. Don't you, Lieutenant?"

"Yes sir! You got yourself an S-5."

The next day, I signed for an Army desk and a Royal typewriter: I had another war now. Of course, I had just been a combat soldier till now. I had been in villages just to search and destroy—to search or destroy them. The malnutrition: I didn't detect it. The skin scabs: I figured, *That's the way kids are in South Vietnam. They're naked, they're dirty, they're cruddy*. The diseases: I suddenly had to have these shown to me. Once, I took an infant to Tamky General Hospital. But the nurse wouldn't let us in: she started to scold the mother badly and told her, "You're a horrible mother! Go home!" The disease: it was nothing but after-birth, it was never washed off, it had rotted away. But once, I took an Army doctor to a Vietnamese village: once, he just wouldn't go a second time. He told me, "I think everyone has tuberculosis here." I flew to Division for those tuberculosis tests: I got four hundred of those little things, and three hundred people had it. For that doctor that was a trauma, I'm sure! As for me, I wasn't a medical personnel, but I realized, *God. They grow up with it. Live with it. Die with it*.

The life there: I started to learn about it. I can't describe it to Americans, it is so unbelievable to us. People who haven't heard of penicillin, merthiolate, aspirin, who haven't the vaguest idea of what bandaids are for. Or what soap's for! One day, I gave a few children bags of it: Lifebuoy, and they thought it was candy bars. And they ripped the wrappers off and—*phooie*, and still continued to eat it. They're people whose whole life is food, defecation, reproduction, and, if they're lucky, land: and that's it. They haven't running water, gas, or electricity, and God knows if you showed them a TV set. It's almost unreal there, and I had been there for months without seeing it. I knew, *I can win if I make these people aware of their prospects.* Of the comforts that a democracy offered them. God, if our society was as great as I thought, the Vietnamese just would gobble it up. And would say, "Let's get it! Let's kick out the communists now! Let's go!"

I had to convince them. But slowly: the Vietnamese are like anyone else and rather would stay in the status quo. It's easier, and I couldn't say, "Sit down, and I'll strip you of it. Your society's screwed up. Your father and your grandfather's screwed up. Buddha's screwed up—" I couldn't: I used a little salesmanship instead. Say if an Arab came to your dinner table to win your heart and mind, someday. You might say, *It's their custom,* but you wouldn't listen if everything he was through with he threw on the floor. Or worse, if he got on your dinner table and he *kicked* everything on the floor: as a GI does. As an S-5, I didn't enter a Vietnamese house if I wasn't asked to. I didn't point at a Vietnamese and say, "Hey, come here," or simply wave at a Vietnamese with my palm up. That's how to wave at animals there, I learned. I didn't call a Vietnamese by his first name: I adopted the Vietnamese ways.

For example: wells. A well in Vietnam is a status symbol, sort of. A man that doesn't need the community well can say, *I have something special.* Now, I had cement and I'd try telling a Vietnamese, "I'm the S-5 here. I can build you a well outside."

"You can't until 1969. Or someone will die."

"Someone will die?"

"And also. It must be *inside* or someone will die."

"Oh, you're just a superstitious idiot—" I didn't say it, I showed the Vietnamese respect. I said, "It can't be inside, or there will be pollution in it. It must be forty feet off." I would explain, or I'd try to.

I felt alive now, as I never had in America. I felt helpful, even if I couldn't build an SST, a spaceship, or something spectacular. I built wells, I showed the Vietnamese movies: I even showed them *The Green Berets*, and I went out to medcap them too. A medcap: that's a short word, *med* is for medical, probably, but *cap*—? I didn't even know. I put merthiolate on bruises, bandages on little skinned toes, and a salve on the skin irritations. At first, I had to cram those medicines down. But soon people saw, *It's free, and I'll give these aspirins to Joe in a VC hospital. Or to the black marketeers.* And then people almost shouted at me, *"Beaucoup hurt."* I wasn't stopping communism: hell, or even diseases,

but I was getting the Vietnamese *to* me. To listen to me: I
had some paper leaflets, or I had pencils, papers, and ABCs
to try to teach reading with. And start a class in Capitalism
soon.

I started a sewing class. I got a German instructor and
five sewing students, some of them prostitutes from the
monkey house: the Vietnamese jail. And five little sewing
machines that the girls could keep to open their sewing
shops with. To compete with: I was teaching the Vietnamese free enterprise. And giving the Vietnamese desires and
telling them, "See? I can better your life." And taking the
Vietnamese from the itty-bitty little paddies there. I saw
some tremendous possibilities now: I saw a tremendous
force of Americans say, "We can help you," I saw the Vietnamese tell us, "You're right. You're treating us now like
human beings. And you're not racists—" I say that because
that's the VC propaganda. To say we carry the race riots everywhere: to Negroes here and to Mongols there. And destroy them: but if we're there to throw silver dollars away,
the Vietnamese will be rushing up and taking them. And
telling us, "You've got the greatest thing going!" And we're
going to win their hearts and minds.

I really believed it. I had a
beautiful thing with the Vietnamese people. Not just with

my interpreter, who even subscribed to *Playboy* and plastered his bedroom with it: but almost everyone, and I would brief the Colonel about it every day. "Good evening, sir."

"Well, Calley? What did the S-5 do?"

"Well, sir—" and I would stand with an Army pencil, pointer, anything, and would say we had demonstrated soap to Vietnamese kids. Or vaccinated their cows, or taken shrapnel out. Or sent to Saigon for fancy diplomas for the sewing class. Or seen about the pigs again.

"Calley, I want to hear about those damned pigs."

"Yes sir—" and I would tell him in two thousand words.

"So how are those pigs?"

"Outstanding, sir."

"Yes, I tell the brigade commander that. But how are those pigs?"

"They're shitty, sir. I'm really upset about it."

"You ought to say so. We could be through hours ago. Be having a drink together. Two!"

I have an important story here. The pigs were starving: dying, and these were all American pigs. We had given them to a Vietnamese farmer free: I don't know if "Ky" is his last name, but he always told me, "Call me Ky." He had raised them, and he had sold those pigs to his neighbors: fine. It was free enterprise. It went against communism. I thought okay: but Ky had told everyone that the pig food, they had to buy from *him*. And now the pigs would be dying, and I asked everyone, "Why?"

"I haven't food."

"Why?"

"I haven't five piasters for Ky."

Now, in Vietnam a pig's almost like a diamond ring. But think of a diamond ring, it loses value if you don't polish it: the pigs needed food, and I had to find it. I briefed the Colonel about it and went around to the mess sergeants. "How is it going, sergeant?"

"Fine, sir."

"I'm the S-5 here. I'm promoting a little bit of human relations with the Vietnamese."

"Yes sir! I'm promoting a little myself."

"And all I want is the wet-waste here." The potato peels, the onion shells, the outer lettuce leaves: the stuff for the garbage cans.

"For the Vietnamese people?"

"For their pigs. I sure would appreciate if you could keep the coffee grounds out of it. And take it and cruise up the road to Hoian. And—"

"Sir? On the road to Hoian there is a laundry shop." A whore house.

"Yes."

"I wear whites, and I could sure use a laundry shop."

"Yes."

"I think that if you could give me—"

"Authorization? Yes."

"I'll do it, Lieutenant!"

So every day, in Hoian there would be ten full garbage

cans. A little less on a Sunday, when we had late breakfast and a Sunday dinner, that's all. And tons whenever the VC hit and put our refrigerators out. The sergeants would drive to Hoian, get a little ass, wine, pot, or whatever, and put all the wet-waste where the Vietnamese people could get it. And still the pigs would be lying down in the shade: dying, and I asked everyone, "Why?"

"I haven't food."

"Why?"

"I haven't five piasters for Ky."

Now, would you believe it? Ky had been taking the garbage cans. And guarding them, and dishing them out in number-ten cans. And selling them all at five cents apiece, and acting as if *I'm king of the pig-food business here.* He had been getting rich on American pigs and American garbage.

I tried talking to Ky myself. I said, "You can't have—"

"You cheat me! No get enough on Sunday! No get enough any day! Is five garbage cans in ten garbage cans, and you put water in. And say, *It is beaucoup food—*"

I just couldn't speak. I thought, *Damn it, I didn't have to give anyone slop. I didn't charge,* but Ky was telling me I had watered it and he had been dipping the water off at five piasters each. He had: except that he had been selling the water, too. I told him, "Ky, you can't do it—"

"I can! I'm the pig man here."

It just isn't right, I thought. I had been showing the Vietnamese how capitalism could—I almost said how "imperialism" could. But that's really it: I had been making the rich people richer, that's all. I had gotten those pigs, and Ky was being a gangster about them. I had built wells, and rich people now were fencing them off. I had helped some of the village chiefs make $100 a day from prostitutes, liquor, and pot. I had helped the Vietnamese people, sure: the greedy ones. The real greedy people went for America big. And they loved us. And depended on us. And even wanted democracy from us. For with democracy, the Vietnamese people would vote for—Ky, and he would be making their laws and be doing worse.

I tried, but I couldn't stop him. I couldn't get a GI to guard garbage cans, or a truck to deliver them to everyone's pig. I told the Colonel, "Sir, I'm upset about it. I'm causing dissension here."

"Do you know how to solve it?"

"No sir."

"Do you know my philosophy?"

"Yes sir."

"And it is—"

"*Solve it.*"

"Yes, that is my philosophy."

In other words: the Colonel couldn't worry about it. Division didn't care: it would ask him, "How many medcaps?" "How many patients?" "How many pigs?" It even would fill in a score card: it wanted statistics, but it would never ask him, "How much dissension now?" Dissension looked bad: *I* had to worry about it. I did: I went to the sergeants, and I said don't send the garbage out. And went to Ky's house a few days later, and god! He had every pig in the village there. He told me, "I got them again," and I had to get them garbage or he would slaughter them. And then market them: American pigs.

I like thinking I'm conscientious. I went to the officers club, I sat on a barstool there, I had a stiff drink: a bourbon, and I thought about things. I had come here to stop communism: to show these people that the American way is a better one. I had believed it: I had been briefed for twenty-five years how America is the greatest there is. Just look at American cars! American houses, and in just eighty years they are paid for! American swimming pools—gosh! A year in Vietnam had just bolstered me. I had just thought, *It's filthy here. It's unsanitary here. The people live in grass houses here—* I never thought, *I can learn something here.* Or why weren't they in America helping *us.*

I had tried changing them. I once heard a colonel say, "Face it. To win here, we've got to tear away their whole way of life." I listened, and I didn't think, *I might as well shoot them.* A life in Asia might not be important: there are a billion there. But their heritage, there's only one. I didn't think that in Vietnam it's death before dishonor, and I had dishonored them: I had booted them. And they might take the boot itself, but America: they didn't want it. Susie didn't want it. Yvonne didn't want it. The old men, women, and children at Mylai didn't want it: I could see why. I had once been in North Dakota. If someone says, "Go back to

North Dakota," I'll become terrified. I'll feel lonely there, but in Dakota they loved it. And the Vietnamese love their society too. A gentle society.

Once, I had looked at a Vietnamese map. And Jesus: I couldn't recognize it. I had thought, *Where in the hell is America?* The center was Asia, and we were on the outer edges. We had to be put together again. We had been split. I had thought, *Oh, the Vietnamese have a screwy map:* I didn't think, *I'm not that great after all.* At last, I had some perspective on us. I saw: in America, it doesn't matter much if you're rich, if only you're richer than the Joneses are. If all you're eating is dried beans, it still doesn't matter much if you're telling the Joneses, "I had four beans today. And you had three: I'm better than you are." Greed: I didn't think this was a good thing for Vietnam to change to. And they didn't think so either. My leaflets: I had kept seeing them as restaurant napkins there, or with fishes inside.

I think we have overrated democracy. I feel now, *Our propaganda, I should crumple it up.* We offer the Vietnamese freedom. What's freedom? We practically offer them the Stars and Stripes Forever. And honeysuckle forever. Lie on the beaches forever— We promise them, "You can do anything."

"I can raise that pig?"

"No, you can do anything! You can have great ambitions! You can be someone tremendous! You can be—"

Bullshit! A farmer in Asia doesn't want to be any nuclear scientist. Or a lawyer, or to use light switches or air condi-

tioners, or to own some commercial crap. And worry about
the Sears bill: no, a utopia to a Vietnamese farmer is a little
land and a healthy pig. Are you sick of the communists?
Well, the Vietnamese aren't. And if I were a Vietnamese
and I wanted that pig, I would go communism rather than
go American Dream.

I left the officers club. And saw the Colonel and told him,
"I'm sorry, sir. You better get another S-5. I'm quitting." I'd
come a hundred and eighty degrees now. I'd come thinking
the Vietnamese were all screaming, "Help, the VC are taking land. And food. And people to VC work camps—" But
they weren't screaming that: the Vietnamese all were
screaming, "Leave us alone!" It just isn't human nature to
help someone who is screaming, "Leave me alone!" Who's
shooting you in the cheek and in the other cheek too. Who's
killing you: it just isn't human nature.

And the GIs there knew it. If they had a druther of going
home and of Vietnam all going communism, most of them
would say, "Jesus! I'm going home!"

I'd like to have helped those
people. I could see so much to do: such tremendous things,
but we have those things in America, too. *We* need schools,
hospitals, houses, we need to have sewing classes if all women
are to support themselves here. We need democracy here.

The whites and the blacks, the North and the South, the laborers and the managers, the Christians and Jews: we still aren't where if you donate labor, or thought, or whatever, you'll reap the rewards in equal proportion. I think if we stay cool, we will achieve it: will share in America's wealth and be a more perfect society. We have to keep working at it. And then we might go to Vietnam and say, "Be like us."

As for me, I've already talked about it: I got orders home in June, 1969, and I was flown right to Washington, the Office of the Inspector General. I wasn't told why: I was for it, though, I was all for investigations. In fact, I wanted to see the whole damn war in Vietnam investigated. And the Army ask, "Is it right or wrong?" We had killed three hundred thousand civilians there, a Senate committee said, we had wounded five hundred thousand more, we had made four million refugees, and I wanted to hear someone ask, "Is it worth it?" We had had search-and-destroy operations every day, we had shot artillery every night, and we had bombed more in Vietnam: in South Vietnam, than in Japan, Germany, Italy, and Korea. And then killed their crops, and I wish the colonel in Washington had asked me, "Lieutenant Calley? This is about the American war in Vietnam." He didn't, though. He said, "This is about an operation on 16 March 1968 in the village of Mylai Four."

I couldn't understand it. An investigation of Mylai? Why not Operation Golden Fleece? Or Operation Norfolk Victory? Or Operation Dragon Valley? Or why not Saigon itself? We had killed hundreds of men, women, and children there in February and March, 1968: in Tet. The colonel didn't have to ask about it: simply read it in *Stars and Stripes*. Or *The New York Times*.

FEBRUARY 3. There has been some resentment about the use of armed helicopters and fighter-bombers in populated areas.

FEBRUARY 4. The suburb looked like Stalingrad today. Row after row of concrete houses had been destroyed. It seemed that many Vietnamese civilians had died.

American jets attacked the area several times. "Love those 500-pound bombs," said a marine adviser.

FEBRUARY 6. Artillery shelled a densely populated area, and a Canadian officer said, "I think Hanoi is a safer place than Saigon this week."

FEBRUARY 7. Planes streaked low. . . .

If you're dead you're dead, and I don't think you'll care if an F-4 or an M-16 did it. Why didn't the Army investigate that?

Why me? The colonel in Washington told me, "It can be murder," and I was charged in September at Fort Benning, Georgia. A colonel read me the specifications with no more emotion than "Well, that's it."

In that First Lieutenant William L. Calley Jr. . . .
In that First Lieutenant William L. Calley Jr. . . .
In that First Lieutenant William L. Calley Jr. . . .

And read them. And read them: I was in shock posture now. I was numb! The colonel could have no malice for me, I knew: *So why would he say these things about me? A hundred and*—I had lost count, I had to ask that colonel, "Sir, can I see those specifications myself?" I had killed people in Mylai: everyone had. But Jesus! A hundred civilians? A hundred would be the body count of my whole platoon and the second, too. It was as though all of Mylai: of Vietnam, was now being blamed on me.

The trial began last November. Each day, I got up at seven-thirty, got dressed, and drove in a Volkswagen to "Calley hall." I thought, *It's a waste of damn camera film,* but I went in the western door for ABC, NBC, and CBS television. Inside, I had coffee: breakfast, and I talked about things with my attorneys. Or with officer friends.

"How goes it?"

"Oh, today they're trying to burn me."

"Hang in."

At nine o'clock sharp, the Judge, an Army full colonel, came by the defense room. And clapped, or whistled, or gestured like a man ringing a dinner bell or reeling a little fish in. "Okay, troops," and I went inside. A beautiful life for an Army officer, really. I couldn't bitch: I sat at a wooden table nine to four-thirty, minus a half-hour coffee break, a two-hour lunch at the officers club, and a half-hour coffee break. I just had to sit straight, to listen to GIs testify, and to keep thinking, *Why would they say it? "Calley did it, Calley, Calley—"*

"I'll ask you," the prosecutor said, "to speak into the microphone. Would you state your full name?"

"Dennis Conti."

"And your present address?"

"Providence, Rhode Island."

"And your occupation?"

"Truck driver."

"Mr. Conti. Have you served in the Army?"

"Yes."

"And do you know the accused?"

"Yes."

"And would you point to him, please, and repeat his name?"

"Lieutenant Calley! Right there!"

The first of the star witnesses was PFC Conti. He had black sideburns and a black mustache now: the fad, I suppose. He sat in a simple witness box. The microphone wire, he twisted and twisted around his left index finger.

"What happened at Mylai Four?"

"The door gunners on the choppers opened up. We hit and everybody jumped out."

"Did you see Lieutenant Calley?"

"No, I met up with Sergeant Bacon."

"Where?"

"Just inside the village. And they were taking potshots at a buffalo there, I guess for sport. And—"

"Don't tell us what you guess," the Judge interrupted him. Conti was interrupted often.

"Okay. Sergeant Bacon told me—"

"Objection."

"Beg pardon," the Judge again.

"Objection."

"To what?"

"Well, the witness, I believe, if I heard correctly, said, 'Sergeant Bacon told me—' "

"Excuse me. How did you start that?"

"I said, 'Sergeant Bacon told me—' "

"All right. Objection sustained."

"Uh—"

"Did you leave the area?"

"Right. I walked up the trail, and I seen Lieutenant Calley. He said to round up the people."

"Objection."

"Who said to round up the people?"

"Lieutenant Calley."

"Overruled," the Judge said.

"—to round up the people, so I went and I found a few people, five or six."

"Could you describe these people?"

"Women and children. From their, I don't know, thirties, down to three four years old."

"Were any of them armed?"

"No."

"What were they doing?"

"Huddling together. Scared, I guess."

"Listen, I told you," the Judge said. "I don't want to hear what you guess. I'm going to strike the 'Scared.' "

"So what did you do with the people?"

"I brought them back to the trail. And there was other people there. Other civilians."

"How many?"

"Oh, I guess thirty. Maybe forty."

"And could you describe these people?"

"All women and children. One old man."

"And what were they doing?"

"Just waiting."

"Was anyone else in the area?"

"Any GIs?"

"Yes."

"The only one I remember was Meadlo."

"So what did you do?"

"Lieutenant Calley come out and told us, 'Take care of the people.' I said, 'All right.' So then he come out—"

"Who?"

"Lieutenant Calley. Then he come out, I don't know, a few minutes later. And said, 'I thought I told you, *Take care of these people.*' I said, 'We are. We're watching them.' And he said, 'No, I meant kill them.'"

"And—?"

"Uh, I was a little stunned, and I didn't know what to do. He said, 'Go get on line and we'll fire.' And they got on line and they opened fire."

"Who?"

"Meadlo and Lieutenant Calley."

"And where did they fire?"

"Into the people."

"How long did they fire?"

"What?"

"How long did they fire?"

"A minute, two minutes."

"And what did the people do?"

"Just screamed and yelled."

"What were the conditions of the people?"

"Uh, pretty messed up. A lot of heads had been shot off. Flesh—uh, fleshy parts of their thighs, their sides, their arms. They were pretty messed up."

"And what condition was Meadlo in?"

"He started crying. He said he couldn't kill the people anymore. And he stuck the weapon in my hand and said, 'You do it.' I said, 'I'm not gonna do it, I'm not gonna do it.' We turned around, and five women and six kids: eleven people were running to the treeline. Uh, Calley said, *Get 'em! Get 'em! Kill 'em—*"

I didn't believe him. To begin with, Conti didn't say it had happened east of Mylai at the irrigation ditch. He said it had happened halfway through, and I knew I wasn't saying then, "Go round the Vietnamese up." I was saying, "Keep going! Keep going!" I knew why Conti wasn't honest, though. It came out on cross-examination.

"You were searching for women, weren't you?"

"No."

"You weren't?"

"No."

"But you did find one, didn't you?"

"No. Not in Mylai Four."

"And you got her— Oh? You found her in another place?"

"This was—uh, later on. Way past Mylai Four."

"Mylai Four! You had a woman down on her knees, didn't you? And you threatened her little baby."

"No."

"You opened your pants and you told her to give you a blow job—"

"I object!"

"—and Lieutenant Calley stopped you. Didn't he?"

"No."

"Mr. Conti. You admired Lieutenant Calley, didn't you?"

"No."

"You thought he was an outstanding leader, didn't you?"

"No."

"You mean you didn't like him, did you?"

"I didn't care for him."

"You hated him, didn't you?"

"No."

"You threatened to shoot Lieutenant Calley, didn't you?"

"No."

"Mr. Conti. Isn't it a fact you'd like to see Lieutenant Calley hang?"

He thought about it three seconds. And then, Conti said, "No."

I knew, *Conti is simply lying about me*. But Meadlo? A perfect soldier, and Meadlo didn't want to hurt me. Or even to testify about me: and didn't until a US marshal sat in. It was testify then or six months' imprisonment, and Meadlo went to the witness chair. He limped: he had that plastic right foot.

"Your name?"

"Paul David Meadlo."

"And your address?"

"Terre Haute, Indiana."

"And your occupation?"

"Slitter operator."

"What?"

"Slitter operator."

"How old are you, Mr. Meadlo?"

"Twenty-three."

"Do you know the accused?"

"Yes."

"Would you point to him and repeat his name?"

"Lieutenant Calley."

And then, Meadlo told the same story that Conti had. The center of Mylai, and thirty to forty people, and old men, women, and children, and "I want them dead." I knew, *Meadlo wouldn't lie*. I figured, *He was just confused that day*.

"What was your condition?"

"I was mortally upset. Scared."

"Were you crying?"

"I imagine I was."

"How long did you remain?" At the center of Mylai.

"Not very long."

"Then where did you go?"

"We just started gathering up more people."

"Where?"

"In hooches and huts."

"How many?"

"Seven or eight."

"Could you describe these people?"

"Men. Women. Children." Meadlo said he had taken them to a ditch: a ravine.

"Where?"

"I don't know."

"Do you know which side of the village?"

"No."

"Were there any Vietnamese there?"

"Yes. There was Vietcong there."

"How many?"

"Seventy-five to a hundred."

"Where were they?"

"Where *were* they?"

"Where were these—"

"By the ravine."

"Inside the ravine?"

"Outside the ravine."

"What happened there?"

"What *happened* there?"

"What did you do?"

"We put all seven or eight with the—uh, the group."

"What were the children doing?"

"I don't remember."

"What were the babies doing?"

"They was in their mothers' arms."

"Had they made any move to attack?"

"I assumed they was getting ready to."

"I move that be stricken as not responsive," the prosecutor said.

"Let that be stricken," the Judge said. "Answer yes or no."

"Had they made any move to attack?"

"Not at that time: no."

"And what was Lieutenant Calley doing?"

"I can't remember."

"What did he say?"

"He said, 'We got another job to do, Meadlo.'"

"So then?"

"Lieutenant Calley started shoving them off and shooting them."

"What did you do?"

"I started shoving them off and shooting them."

"Where were you?"

"At the ravine."

"And where was Lieutenant Calley?"

"By the ravine."

"How deep was the ravine?"

"I don't know."

"Was it over their heads?"

"I can't remember."

"How wide was the ravine?"

"I can't remember."

"How did you fire?"

"I can't remember."

"How did he fire?"

"I can't remember."

"Did you change magazines?"

"Yes."

"Did Lieutenant Calley change magazines?"

"Yes."

"How many times?"

"Between ten and fifteen."

"How many persons were with you?"

"Five or six."

"Did you see Stanley?"

"Yes."

"What was he doing?"

"I believe he was firing."

"Did you see Conti?"

"Yes."

"Do you know what he was doing?"

"I believe he was firing."

"Did you see Simone?"

"Yes."

"And what was he doing?"

"I believe he was firing."

"Did you have conversation with Dursi?"

"Yes."

"Could you relate that?"

"I object," my attorney said.

"This is between you and Dursi?" the Judge said.

"Yes."

"I don't see how that's admissible," the Judge said.

"He can relate what *he* said," the prosecutor said.

"I don't think so," the Judge said.

"Sir, it wouldn't be hearsay."

"No, but I would sustain the objection."

"Was Dursi firing into the people?"

"No."

"Could you describe the people?"

"They was just laying there."

"In what condition?"

"In what condition? Just laying there."

"Where were the wounds?"

"I can't say."

"Can you say what part of the body?"

"Head, stomach, chest."

"Was there blood?"

"Yes."

"What parts of the body?"

"I've stated that."

"Mr. Meadlo. You testified, 'I was very emotional.' Could you describe the emotion?"

"I said I was scared."

"Of carrying out the orders?"

"Of carrying out the orders."

"Why?"

"Why was I afraid?"

"Yes."

"No one really wants to take a human life."

"But they were VC, weren't they?"

"Yes, they were VC."

"That was your job, wasn't it?"

"That was my job."

"And did you receive that order from Captain Medina or Lieutenant Calley?"

"From Lieutenant Calley."

"No further questions."

"*But—*"

"Go ahead," the Judge told him.

"Captain Medina. He knew there was killing going on! Why didn't he put a stop to it?"

"No further questions."

We cross-examined him. Mead-lo said, "I was emotional," "I was under emotional strain," "I

got emotionally upset," and I believe it. Meadlo was just be-
wildered about it. One hundred people. And fifteen clips.
Or three hundred rounds. The next witness said it was
twenty to thirty people and two ammunition clips.

"Your name."

"My name is Charles Sledge."

"And your address?"

"Sardis City." In Mississippi.

"And your occupation?"

"I work as a case sealer at Sardis Luggage Company."

"How old are you, Mr. Sledge?"

"I'm twenty-three years old."

"Are you married?"

"Yes sir."

"Would you raise your voice, please? Do you know the
accused?"

"Yes."

"And would you point to him and repeat his name."

"Lieutenant William Calley."

"Did you know Lieutenant Calley in March, 1968?"

"Yes sir."

"How did you know Lieutenant Calley?"

"He was my platoon leader, and I was his RTO."

"For the record, what is an RTO?"

"A radio telephone operator."

Weber, the RTO and the GI closest to me, had been
killed back in February, remember. In Mylai, Sledge had
become the GI beside me. I knew, *He didn't dislike me. He*

wasn't emotional there. He wouldn't lie. And yet, Sledge testified as Conti and Meadlo had. A third into Mylai, and thirty to forty people, and old men, women, and children, and I supposedly said to Meadlo, "Waste them." But for Sledge, I didn't fire at those people myself. I did at the irrigation ditch.

"And what did the people do?"

"They started falling. And screaming."

"How long did they fire?"

"Not very long."

"And then what?"

"A helicopter landed."

"And then what?"

"Lieutenant Calley went over. And started talking to the helicopter pilot."

"And then what?"

"Lieutenant Calley came back. And said something like, 'He don't like the way I'm running this show, but I'm the boss.'"

"How did he say it?"

"In anger."

"Then what did the helicopter do?"

"Took off."

"Then what did you do?"

"We started moving up the ditch, like. We came up onto a priest—"

"A what?"

"A priest."

"How did you know that he was a priest?"

"He was dressed like a priest. In white."

"What was he doing?"

"Just standing there."

"Where?"

"Up where the ditch made an L shape."

"What did you do?"

"Nothing, but Lieutenant Calley started interrogating. He started asking, '*Vietcong adai*,' but the priest would say, '*No bitt*,' and he would take—"

"Go ahead."

"And he would take his palms and would bow his head."

"Let the record reflect that the witness placed the palms of his hands together and he moved forward," the prosecutor said. "And so?"

"He was just saying, '*No bitt*.' And then, he hit him with the butt of his rifle."

"Where?"

"In the mouth."

"What did the priest do?"

"He sort of felled back, and he started doing this again. Sort of like pleading."

"How old was this individual?"

"He looked about forty or fifty."

"So then what?"

"Lieutenant Calley took his rifle and pulled the trigger."

"Where?"

"In the priest's face."

"What did the priest do?"

"He felled."

"And what happened to the priest's head?"

"It was blown off. It was blown away."

"What's the next thing you recall?"

"Someone hollered, 'There is a child!' You know, running back to the village. Lieutenant Calley ran back and he grabbed it."

"How far was this?"

"From where I was standing?"

"Yes."

"I guess twenty, maybe thirty, feet."

"What did you do?"

"Just stood there."

"Could you describe the child?"

"A little child. About one, maybe two, years old."

"How did he pick it up?"

"By the arms."

"And what did he do?"

"Swung it into the ditch."

"And what did he do?"

"Fired."

"And where did he fire?"

"Into the ditch."

"How many shots?"

"One."

"And how far away were you?"

"About twenty to thirty feet."

"I object," my attorney said. "We're getting repetitive testimony."

"Overruled."

And really, I seemed like a mad killer now. A monster: I loved killing men, women, children, babies, and Buddhist priests. CALLEY KILLS BABY, I knew what those thirty reporters would say. All they wanted in Georgia were the bodies with the blood dripping off or the brains out of someone's head: the Monster stories. At times, I wanted to shake their hands and say, "I hope I'm not slimy today." Even *The New York Times*: the *Times* man didn't try to know me, didn't even talk to me. He just wrote, "As the details of the slaughter of Vietnamese were related, the Lieutenant broke into a grin that lasted for—" It sells papers, I suppose.

But Sledge. I just didn't understand it. He had nothing against me, Sledge: no reason to hurt me. It came out on cross-examination that he had been imprisoned once: for a couple years as a Peeping Tom. I say that means nothing. A black man in Mississippi? Seen out in someone's alley? Hell, I say that's nothing but Sledge's race. I sat there, I listened, and I could only say, *He is wrong about me.* Or could it be, I was wrong instead? I just didn't know.

The last prosecution witness was James Joseph Dursi. Who told me, "I like little kids, and

I can't tell them, *Go away*." He was working now as a tool-room attendant at Western Electric in Brooklyn, New York. He had some sideburns and a mustache too: I knew why. He had been in a lonely war. He just didn't want the loneliness anymore.

"So what did you do?"

"We moved the people in."

"How did you do it?"

"Pushing."

"And what was Meadlo doing?"

"Crying, and pushing the people the same way I was."

"And then what happened?"

"There was an order to shoot."

"By whom?"

"Lieutenant Calley."

"What did he say?"

"Something like 'Start firing.' "

"So then what happened?"

"Lieutenant Calley and Meadlo started firing."

"Continue."

"Meadlo turned to me a couple of minutes after and told me, 'Shoot.' "

"What did Meadlo say?"

"He said, 'Shoot! Why don't you fire?' "

"How did he say this?"

"He was crying and yelling to me."

"And what did you do?"

"I said, 'I can't, I won't.' And looked at the ground."

"What were the people doing?"

"They were screaming, crying, diving on top of each other, the mothers trying to protect the children."

"And when the firing ceased?"

"I saw a lot of blood."

"From what parts of the bodies?"

"Chests. Arms. Some head wounds."

"Mr. Dursi?"

"Yes sir?"

"Why did you not fire?"

"I couldn't. These were defenseless men, women, and kids."

"No more questions."

Dursi would be the last witness the prosecutor would have. And when he had testified direct, and cross, and redirect, and recross: when he was done, he came right out of the courtroom to the defense room. He told me, "No hard feelings, sir."

It may surprise you. But most of those witnesses had been coming there: the defense room. We had been through a war together: through hell, we had stood up for each other knowing that we could easily die. We had been close, and in Georgia we still related as old friends do. I saw those guys, and I couldn't help it: I said, "How are you!" And they weren't embarrassed anymore, and they didn't have it: the terrified look in their eyes. And they told me, "I'm with you," "I hope you get out," "I hope I didn't hurt you, sir."

"Just don't call me *sir*. I'm working for you now—sir."

"Aw, Lieutenant. I'll whip your ass if you call me *sir*."

And so, Dursi came by the defense room too. He seemed sorry, and I didn't want him to torment himself about this day. And tell himself, *I sold someone down the river—god.* He had sworn I had shot about twenty or thirty people in Mylai and fifteen more at the irrigation ditch. And that I had told him, "We have another job to do. Start firing." I didn't know why he had said those things: I wished that he hadn't, but it was water over the dam now. I asked him, "Are you free tonight?"

"I'm leaving tomorrow."

"Come for a drink then." It shouldn't surprise you: I had asked most of the prosecution witnesses home. And they had come.

"All right."

"We better not go together, though. They," I said, and I meant the newspaper people, "will say, *It's conspiracy.*"

"All right."

We got together later. And talked together of GI friends: of old times together. My girl friend didn't understand it: Dursi and I coming home. She told me, "It seems incongruous. He crucifies you and you say, 'Come for a bourbon.'" She's right, I suppose, but I enjoyed it: a college reunion, sort of. Dursi had already told me, "No hard feelings," and I wanted to say something like it. But also, I wanted to see what motivated him. To sit on the witness stand and to say those things.

"My attorney," I said. "I hope he wasn't too hard on you."

"No."

"That's his job. To try to demolish you."

"Yes." He sat there. He sipped from a very small shot of Jim Beam. "You know there's no hard feelings: I've nothing against you."

"I know."

"I had to say it. I got here, and I had to stick to that story—"

"I know."

"—so other people wouldn't be hurt."

"I respect you," I said. "I want to keep other people clean."

I understood it. Dursi wasn't the first one to say it, I knew. A sergeant told me, "I didn't want to testify against you. But others, I had to protect them." The others: I think that was Dursi's motive now. And Sledge's, and Meadlo's, and Conti's, and I think that was the Army's too. It had been headline news, the Mylai assault, and *Life* had those color photographs of it. A screaming woman. A crying child. A row of dead women, children, and babies halfway into Mylai. And the American government couldn't say, "Oh, that's how it is in Vietnam, everyone." It had to protect two million veterans and two hundred million citizens. It had to tell everyone, "A mad killer did it."

I don't even ask, "Why me?" In the Army there isn't a day there isn't a man singled out. "Sergeant, the Army's retreating today. Stay here. Slow the enemy down. And die." The sergeant won't say, "But sir. Why me?" I know as I lay in the paddies with the Vietnamese shooting at me, I didn't say, "Oh, why was I ever born? Why me?" I lived, I got home again, and I had the Army harping on me. And asking everyone, "Where was Lieutenant Calley in Mylai?" "Where did he go?" "What did he do?" I had the Army circling me: I knew, *It isn't right, but I shouldn't say, "Why me? Why me?"* Why not?

I didn't have an ill feeling for Dursi. Hell, I knew how he —how everyone, had been badgered for eighteen months by Army investigators: by IG or Inspector General's Corps, by CID or Criminal Investigations Division, by JAG or Judge Advocate General's Corps, by Peers committee investigators. By congressmen, too: by people who wanted the answers, the right ones. I can imagine it.

"Where was Lieutenant Calley?"

"I don't know."

"But then where were you?"

"I was here."

"Did you see Calley there?"

"No."

"Did you see Calley *wasn't* there?"

"No."

"But wouldn't you see Calley wasn't there if he wasn't there?"

"What?"

"But wouldn't you see Calley wasn't there if he wasn't there?"

"I guess I would."

"You didn't, though."

"I guess I didn't."

"So you saw Calley there."

"I guess I did."

"All right. What was Calley doing there?"

I mean it: a witness who is a law student told me, "I couldn't take it. I'd almost say anything to have gotten out." Another had to have three marijuana cigarettes during it: I have an affidavit saying so. Another drank gin, a full colonel giving him it. He testified so.

At times, the Army went too far. And would then get a statement like,

> I took over as RTO for LIEUTENANT CALLEY. I was to receive any and all radio transmissions for CALLEY. I stayed right beside CALLEY. . . .
>
> Just before we went in, CALLEY informed his men, I believe 1st platoon, that we were supposed to kill everybody. CALLEY. . . .

The soldier signed it. And soon had to sign another one,

> I wish to clarify the statement I furnished. I was the RTO for LIEUTENANT BROOKS, Platoon leader, 2d platoon. I was not the RTO for LIEUTENANT CALLEY.

In fact, there were no two answers alike: a Conti swore that I fired single shot, a Meadlo swore that I fired automatic, a Sledge swore that I didn't fire in the center of Mylai. I fired at the ditch for a minute, two minutes, three minutes, or a whole hour, a GI said. No matter: the answer would be locked in, and either the GI repeated it in Georgia or saw himself up for perjury. Or worse: up for some murders in Mylai himself. So a GI would sit on the stand thinking, *He's innocent. He did what everyone else did in Mylai: actually less. I don't want to hurt those others, though. It's either him or us. Or me—*

"I know," I said to Dursi. "I want to keep other people clean."

"I had to say it, Lieutenant."

"I know," I said to Dursi. "I respect you," I was just bullshitting him. I didn't want Dursi to tell himself, *I saved myself, but I put someone else in a gas chamber then,* if I could relieve his conscience, fine. I gave him my telephone number, I said to Dursi, "Call me," and that ended that. He left.

I don't think of Dursi—of anyone, as wanting to really see me "get" it. The other way around: the American people want to keep looking good. I always hated this: I knew someone in Miami, he always would tell me how rotten everyone was. I'd be in high school and "Gee. Look at Joe over there. He uses Gleem toothpaste. He uses Score: he is really screwed up." I would think, *So what?* Of what relevance is it? Is he just telling me, "I'm better than he is"? He really has an inferiority complex then, or a guilt one. And the American people do if they really want a goat, a pigeon, a patsy.

A Christ. I heard of a play about me: *Pinkville,* the actor comes to the front and center saying, "I will not die for your sins again." I agree with him: I am not a Christ, and if I can stay that way I'm going to. It may be wretched of me: America asks for a Christ, and I'm not willing to be it. I tremendously want to live, though: I'm happy here. I'm sure the world's getting better now. Men at last realize, *We have to live together.* All of this revolution now: I'm for it. Women's lib, black lib, and the revolution against war: I want to watch it. I know, the Cross would be a good vantage point for it. High above everything, but I'd rather be where the crowds are: I'd rather be going through it and helping it through. Or be up there directing it, but that isn't what you're telling me. You're telling me, "Die there."

No thank you. In five minutes there will be someone behind me. Ask *him*: I am meek little me, I wouldn't have the right to die for your sins if I wanted to. I am not worthy: I should be a son of God for that privilege. Or it should go to someone famous: to Hubert Humphrey. President Nixon. President Johnson! I think he would be better suited for it. He has this tremendous air, President Johnson. He would be just ideal: he started the whole damn war, he should stay with it— No. I'm not being nice. I don't wish to see anyone hurt: or anyone die for anyone else's sins. Not President Johnson or General Westmoreland or Captain Medina: I don't want to defame anyone to defend myself. I'm sorry about it: sometimes, my attorneys did to Medina what the prosecutor would do to me. "Now, wasn't the real villain in Mylai Captain Medina? And not the poor sweet lieutenant?" But the lieutenant wasn't all so sweet, and the captain was no more villain than any American from the President down. The guilt: as Medina said, we all as American citizens share it.

I agree. I don't believe in goats, in pigeons, or patsies. I just don't believe they're in America's interest. For years, we Americans all have taken the easy way out. And been hypocritical fools. And gone around saying, "I'm nice. I'm sweet. I'm innocent."

"You starved a thousand people today."

"Who me?"

"You threw away the scraps from the dinner table."

"Aw—"

"You killed a thousand people today."

"*Who me?*"

"You sent the Army to Mylai and—"

"That wasn't me! That was Lieutenant Calley!"

No, that isn't right for America. I say if there's guilt, we must suffer it. And learn. And change. And go on. For that is what guilt must be really for.

The government had on sixty-two witnesses, and we had forty-four on, including me. The prosecutor said, "Gentlemen, it is not your function to resolve the guilt or innocence of any other person in Mylai

Four." My own attorney said, "This wasn't a one-man carnage."

The jury went out on March 16, 1971, the third anniversary of Mylai. It left without having heard from one Vietnamese man, Vietnamese woman, or Vietnamese child: I say that's tragic. Only the Vietnamese really know it: Mylai, the pain of it. The mothers, the fathers, the sisters, the brothers, I know a little about them, I read about them in *One Morning in the War*, by Richard Hammer. One rice farmer in Mylai was Pham Phon. On that morning he, his wife, his sons, and his daughter had gone towards the GIs saying, "Hello! Hello!" And were taken out to the irrigation ditch. Pham Phon:

> I saw a lot of people there. One hundred—but who can count at such a time.
> I tell my wife and my kids: slip in when GI not looking. So then the GI shoot at the standing people and at the sitting people. They fall in and cover us. So we were not wounded: myself, my wife, and my sons. My little daughter, seven years old. . . .
> I am too illiterate to know why it happened.

In war, the dead people really don't cry. The ones who are still alive do. Nguyen Chi:

> I saw a wounded baby. An old lady told me, "You must help the baby." I was too busy. In the canal, I find my husband.

We are a miserable people. And now I must raise my children, and I have no husband anymore. It is war. It is just war.

It is. Americans like to think that war is John Wayne. To get a grenade and a VC's throat, to shove the grenade right down it. Americans sit at television sets and say, "One hundred bodies. Boy!" And they think, *Great*, and they think that I'm the ugly one. I tell you, a hundred bodies still are a hundred people, and if they're dead their guts are just hanging out. And that's pretty horrible: I had once thought, *Oh, war is hell*. And then I saw war, and I could only sit and cry. And ask, *Why did I do it?* Why didn't I stand on a corner and say, "It's wrong." Why didn't I burn my draft card, and I wouldn't have had to go?

I didn't know. I was just an American who was put together with a philosophy: democracy's right. And there was no gray and white, no beige and white, no other colors: there was just black or white, and I was to kill someone if his philosophy's wrong. In school I had never thought about it, communism. I knew the Lord's Prayer, *Our father, etcetera*, and I knew, *Communism's bad*. I wasn't like the Miami girl who talked about it, Mary. Once, I was at a birthday party and I heard her say, "It's worth evaluating. The poverty there is ten percent less—" Or twenty percent less, I didn't listen. I thought, *I've better things to do*. Like dancing, drinking, and raising hell, and I asked another girl, "Let's dance." If communism wasn't bad, I didn't want to hear about it. Americans believe in ancestors too: if our mother, our father, and everyone say, "Niggers are bad," or

"Communism's bad," we believe them. It's law. It's God. Or should be, except we were in Vietnam: in the midst of communism, and we saw nothing bad. And became afraid. And had to destroy it.

I'm different now. I said a long while ago, if Americans tell me, "Go massacre one thousand communists," I will massacre one thousand communists. No longer: today if Americans said, "Go to Mylai. Kill everyone there," I would refuse to. I'd really say, "It's illegal, and I can't be a part of it." Of course, to kill everyone in Mylai isn't the only illegal thing we do. To evacuate them is illegal too: is against the Geneva convention, I've learned. Is kidnapping them. To burn their houses is very illegal, and I don't know why the Judge didn't say, "A reasonable man would realize it: *One shouldn't burn a Vietnamese village.* It is against the Uniform Code of Military Justice, Article CIX." It doesn't carry death, but it does carry five years at Leavenworth. Hell, to just *be* in Mylai with an M-16 and some ammunition is illegal too. You may say, "It isn't a dumdum round." It tears like a dumdum, though. It takes out a VC's organs in a way that's against the Geneva convention. I now think, to go to Vietnam is illegal too.

To go to war anywhere. As for me, I went to Vietnam believing, *I will stop communism. And there will be no one ever to hurt us. And there will be No More War.* I think every man in Vietnam—in history thought, *I'll go and there will be No More War.* And thought this in World War II and World War I and Rome, I suppose. And died in vain every time: I say that's immoral. A war that isn't the world's last war, I say that's illegal: or we shouldn't call the Army the Peace Force. At times, I read about war in the year 2000, and I'm just sickened by it. Laser rays. And infrared rays. And robots: for God's sake, why go on fighting these wars? I don't understand it. Peace, is that what you're after? All right: to establish it, just abolish war. A little intelligence, and I say America can do it. Our money on goddamn going to Mars—or on munitions, if I had that money I could do it.

It isn't enough when the President says, "No more troops." And says to use bombers, artillery pieces, and even lasers instead. And never thinks, *Who's at the end of that laser beam?* It's some other soldier, that's who, or some civilian. I saw a Pentagon statement once:

> Some exciting horizons. We can detect anything that perspires, moves, carries metal, makes a noise, or is hotter or colder than its surroundings. The potential: the instrumentation of the entire battlefield. A "year 2000" vision. . . .

Now, listen: a Vietnamese civilian perspires, moves, carries metal, makes a noise, and is hotter or colder than his surroundings. If he's blind, he perspires, moves—the instrument knows this, but it doesn't know, *I'm doing evil.* Do you know those automatic automobile washes? The water? The soapsuds? The scrubbers? And everyone says, "It has cleaned the car. It's great." It would do the same to a duck truck, though. Or a bicycle, or a tricycle, or a baby carriage:

give you a very clean baby, but a very dead one, too. The same in a "year 2000" war. An instrument wouldn't care if a Vietnamese is young, old, paraplegic, man, woman, or child. As we didn't care at Mylai.

Well. The jury went out on March 16, 1971. It deliberated all the week and the next. It sent notes out: to get grease pencils or to get hours of testimony read. I waited in my apartment here on Arrowhead road. I couldn't sleep: I stayed up till seven o'clock making statues of papier maché, and I drank. I had a thousand thoughts then: if I was depressed, if I was worried, if I was really uptight, I thought, *Damn. What if they didn't believe me? And say, "You're a lowlife killer! You should die!"* And other times I thought, *I was charged.* To be guilty—hell, it wouldn't hurt me any worse, it wouldn't make me cry or embarrass me or make me scream any louder. If they're worthless enough to hang me, I should care? I didn't know how I'd be being hanged: I guess like a child, screaming. I thought, *I'd love being brave,* and I saw myself on the gallows saying, "Well, everyone, screw you!" Then going through, and an echoing word in the courtyard would be "Geronimo." And *gulp,* and that's it: I wouldn't give a good goddamn.

But other times I thought, *No, I have prospects now.* I knew in Vietnam three years ago, *America is a damn steamroller here.* We kill a Vietnamese's wife and I tell him, "I'm sorry." And ask at Division for a $10 solace allowance. And tell it, "We're getting increasingly deadly—"

"We're aware of it. Nice seeing you."

Ironic: I had an audience now, I now could talk and be listened to. Some people said, "He shouldn't be tried: simply hanged." And some people said, "No, he should be tried. As long as he is hanged afterwards." And some people went the whole other way, too. I didn't care: I knew, *They'll listen to me*. I had visions then: I'll get out, I'll talk everywhere in America, and I'll tell it I'm one little finger of a Frankenstein monster. A probe that it sent to Vietnam that is home now to tell it, "No More War."

I have those visions still: for I am still here on Arrowhead road and it still isn't in, the jury. The actual jury: the President, and the American people. I wish I had a pat vocabulary now. If only my jaw would react to my brain or if—! This is spontaneous now: I wish the American people would say, "We aren't Almighty God." And would look at the blacks and the Jews and the yellow race and the Buddhists and say, "And what do I have that is any better?" As for me, I like Christianity. A man could tell me, "It isn't true. It's really a spoof and—" I wouldn't care. I still enjoy it: I know, *I'm happy with it*. A man with a little paddy says, "I like something else, and I'm happy too." I ask would communism hurt him? It wouldn't hurt him a damned bit! Compared to a war, communism would be a godsend.

No war anymore: I'm optimistic about it. America is a brave nation. And we'll say, "All right. We believe this. If you don't, fine. We will live happily." I see it so vividly! I think of our fifty thousand dead, I think of their million dead: I think of the bodies in Mylai Four. All rotting, and I think, *Can there be any good from it?* Maybe there can. The horrors of war came together at Mylai on March 16, 1968. And maybe someday the GIs who went there will say, *Now the world knows what war is. And now the world really hates it. And now there is No More War.*